A CALL

FROM THE

21ST

CENTURY

THE TECHNOLOGY OF CUSTOMER CONTACT

Is it a fact – or have I dreamt it – that, by means of electricity, the world of matter has become a great nerve, vibrating thousands of miles in a breathless point of time?

– *NATHANIEL HAWTHORNE,*
The House of the Seven Gables (1851)
inspired by the development of the telegraph

A CALL
FROM THE
21ST
CENTURY

THE TECHNOLOGY OF CUSTOMER CONTACT

PAUL ANDERSON

 *Doyle Publishing Company*

Published by
Doyle Publishing Company
5222 FM 1960 West, Suite 112
Houston, Texas 77069 USA
1-800-457-6459

Publisher's Cataloging in Publication
Anderson, Paul, 1964-
    A call from the 21st century: the technology of customer contact / Paul Anderson.
        p. cm.

        1. Telecommunication–Forecasting. 2. Telecommunication–Technological innovations. 3. Information technology. I. Title.

    HE 7631.A64 1997   384–ddc20   96-071809

ISBN 0-9653359-0-9

Cover design by Decoz
Book design by Momentum Printing & Graphics
Printed in the United States of America
First printing: 1997

Thanks

Nothing can be made to be of interest to the reader that was not first of vital concern to the writer. Each writer's prejudices, tastes, background and experience tend to limit the kinds of character, actions and settings, he can honestly care about, since by the nature of our mortality we care about what we know and might lose (or have lost), dislike that which has no visible bearing on safety of the people and the things we love. Thus no two writers get aesthetic interest from exactly the same materials. Mark Twain, saddled with a cast of characters selected by Henry James, would be quick to maneuver them all into wells.
– John Gardner, The Art of Fiction

With Love to Cheryl, Kyle and the whole family.

Thanks to everyone on my procrastination short list that I called when I needed to stall, or needed a good idea or two. Thanks to Kevin C. for five years of excellent Word for Windows instruction. The old guys Larry D., Richard L., Bob & Marilyn K., Cliff E., Craig Sensei & Houston Budokan, John I., Hans K., Allan T., Art R., Tom S., John & M.E. Nelson, John G., John U., Mike D., Diane K., Judy L., Scott Peterson, Robert Fletcher, Carol Beesley, Michele Arnold, Nicholas Negroponte, and Sir Peter & Lady Jill Duchon.

Special thanks to:
Barry Thomas, Stuart White, Irving Wyble. Niels, for all of your help keeping this project from going up in smoke, right when I needed it most. Cover art by Hans Decoz.

Very special thanks to:
Howie Doyle, Treva Bedinghaus, and especialy Lynn Alperin.

There is only one thing better than to have a friend that you can trust, and that is a friend who will trust you. My sincerest thanks and appreciation goes to Gail.

Thanks,
Paul V. Anderson

CONTENTS

PREFACE

Restlessness and discontent are the necessities of progress.
— Tom Edison

Communication sustains cultures, societies, and economies. Without implicit communication, how else could we find meaning in a seemingly meaningless, often brutal, and alienating world? The answer is that we gain meaning by infusing our tasks with a sense of purpose and by seeking human connection to communicate that purpose. The restlessness and discontent that accompany technological progress come from a burgeoning cultural fear of a void of "unconnectedness." We, as human beings, have spent almost our entire evolution developing unique tools with which to connect and communicate.

The atom may be the single icon that best represents 20th century science and technology. The atom whirls alone, the epitome of singleness. A continent, a nation, a city-state, and an individual can be represented by the atom. Symbolizing potential, knowledge, and uncertainty, the atom conveys the naked power of simplicity. However, almost as quickly as a tachyon burst in a particle accelerator, the iconic reign of the atom appears to be passing; a new metaphor and symbol for science in the next century has arrived: the dynamic Internet.

An Internet, as opposed to the atom, has no center. The Internet consists of a bunch of dots connected to dots. This icon is an archetype

1

displayed to represent all circuits, all intelligence, and interdependence. The Internet conveys the logic of both the computer and nature. In nature, the Internet finds form in, for example, the beehive. The hive is unabashedly of many minds, but it decides as a whole when to swarm and where to move. A hive possesses a collective intelligence that none of its parts has.[1] And so does man.

But the hive of mankind has not yet become unified. We couldn't swarm together if we tried. As information technology becomes more important for economic success and social interconnectedness, the divisive existence of an "information apartheid" becomes increasingly real. Despite the glamour of technology, the wholesale automation generated by technology is tending to accelerate a dangerous polarization, fragmentation, and splintering of our society. A growing cleavage is growing between the digital "haves" and the digital "have-nots." This book is about and for the digital "haves"; I do not, however, discount the digital "have-nots." Quite the contrary. I think that technologists would do well to pay attention to the tremendous population of digital "have-nots" who will affect the ensuing generation. However, this is the subject of whole other disciplines that have manifested themselves in such extreme radicals as the Unabomber and the Luddites.

As a society, we are approaching the end of the Industrial Age tunnel. We can certainly make out the blinding light of the digital future some distance ahead, but we are currently in the no man's land in between. Considering that the future itself is barely visible, can we be surprised that most of the ideas about it are blurry?[2]

It pays to see what is coming down the road. We all have a vested interest in knowing what the future holds for us. Forecasts have always been big business, in spite of their short life spans. But, forecasting the future is difficult. Predictions of transformation prove rarely to be accurate, and the proof of the value can only be found in the results.

Deciphering the easiest way to meet the technological challenges of the next five years requires a keen sense of the obvious. And even with the obvious, you may be heading in the right direction, but in the wrong lane (the Law of Life's Highway). As far as any type of technology is concerned, now is not the time to overcommit to some unpredictable, future endgame.

With new digital technologies emerging faster than the marketplace can absorb them, no intelligent forecaster can fixate on any single end point. The digital revolution is a process, not a product, and this revolution is evolutionary and proceeds, often fitfully, along an unpredictable path. As I was going to press with this book in August, 1996, AT&T scientists had recently demonstrated the transmission of one trillion bits of data – in a single second. In just one second, the equivalent amount of information printed in more than 300 years of every daily newspaper flew down multiple streams of fiber optic, bit-bearing light! The amazing thing is that this capability was not predicted to be available until long after the year 2000!

Can we grasp how large a number one trillion is? If 11 days contain one million seconds, and 31 years contain one billion seconds, one trillion seconds count back almost 30,000 years before the birth of Christ!

Even in the world of the digital "haves," a tremendously huge gap exists between the unlimited bandwidth of fiber optics in the laboratory and existing services ready for the masses. Many companies have wised up to the fact that they must have a critical interest in what and how they communicate with their stakeholders. This book is intended to serve that interest.

Before I jump into technology and communication, let me point out before my critics do that, as a technologist, I am woefully undigital. I have no pager; no cellular phone; no cable for my wife's giant diamond-screen TV; no CNN, ESPN, or technology channel; no home theater system; and no hi-fi stereo. I rarely surf the Internet, and I really cannot program my own VCR. I have to keep my house alarm code the same as my voicemail code so that I will not forget either. I write about phones all of the time, but I cannot even fix mine when it is broken. A Compaq 486 with Windows 3.11 suits me just fine, and I still have to hire a rent-a-genius to fix my PC when anything half-bad goes wrong. Saying that I just like to read feels almost anachronistic. I am a typical consumer, inundated with more technology than I can handle.

Because this is ultimately a book about the never-ceasing morph of technology and how we use it to engage each other, I have tried to be accurate and timely with the facts used. In the process I have concluded that this is nearly impossible when writing about technology. Writing about technology carries inherent dangers, and I apologize in advance for any apparent statistical misrepresentations or factual mischaracterization. If you have an opinion regarding technology and make the mistake of writing about it, time has a peculiar way of either embarrassing or vindicating you. Because the universe tends toward perversity in outcomes, the writer is usually embarrassed. I still have a twinge of fear that my critics will accuse me, as the futurist Paul Saffo remarked ignominiously about George Gilder, when he said, " The problem with advocates like Gilder is that they use facts like a drunk uses a lamppost – for support rather than for illumination." I am prepared.

I have discovered that either you can write about technology or you can write about trends, but you cannot describe both at the same time with any degree of accuracy. The reason, oddly enough, lies in an axiom of quantum physics called the Heisenberg Uncertainty Principle.

The Heisenberg Principle states that, at a quantum level, light demonstrates both particle and wave forms, depending on the way you look at it. Atoms can be either a particle or a wave but not both, and some properties of atoms and their particles – such as position and linear momentum – can be determined simultaneously only to within a certain degree of accuracy. In other words, we cannot measure the position and the momentum of a particle at the same time. Just the process of measuring the particle's position disturbs the momentum, and vice versa (this is as scientific as this book gets). For example, attempting to measure accurately the position of an atom by viewing that atom with an ideal microscope demonstrates the theory. After light interacts with the atom, that atom can be analyzed to determine its position. The light, however, imparts also momentum to the atom.

Why would most technology-oriented people, particularly those in telecommunications, be interested in quantum physics? The Uncertainty Principle, in its statement of the limits of observation, is a part of the present scientific view of the nature of physical reality, with deep implications for philosophy in general. I prefer to stay out of the illusory world of the theoretical, however, and apply this principle to the more real and concrete world of the technology we use to communicate, specifically through the amalgamated technologies found in call centers.

After all, phone calls, in all of their variations, model precisely what networked markets are all about – the information economy. Ironically, call center technology mirrors nature in a fundamental sense. That is, the more closely you try to define, name, and describe the term "call center," the harder it becomes. The spectrum of definitions is broad. At one extreme, the term refers to the type of formal call centers run by Wells Fargo and Microsoft. At the other extreme, it refers to a small cluster of interconnected, nomadic or home-based workers. As with nature, we can either talk about the big picture of call centers, the trends, or we can discuss the specific technologies found in the call centers; but we cannot discuss both at the same time. Hence, the format of this book: one half, trends, and the other half, technology.

Giant organizations with huge numbers of products and customers are struggling already with a competitive situation that is becoming so complex their current product-management and marketing organizations do not seem equal to the task. Smaller, leaner, faster-growing organizations quickly get the jump on the giants, not because they are quicker and more flexible but because they are so much closer to their customers. As a result, some of those megacompanies are now locked in soul-searching efforts to turn themselves into more fluid, customer-oriented structures. In effect, many are trying to evolve into networks of quasi-independent, small organizations.[3] They are mimicking the networking of the iconic Internet.

In my travels to research and interview for this book, I often found call center professionals quickly willing to say, "Well, it's obvious to me that . . . is what's going to happen in the next few years." But, stating the obvious is often not so facile as it may appear. For example, when watching a seasonal flock of flying geese migrating in their customary V-shape formation, do you know why one leg of the "V" is longer than the other? The "obvious" answer: There are more geese in the longer leg.

Forecasting anything, particularly in the realm of telecommunications technology, is less simple and not so obvious. The forecaster must study a myriad of influences, many not even seemingly related technically. A random selection of any page in the first half of this book may find you reading about the economy, the telephone, client/server architecture, management of the human work force, the Internet, on-line banking, or the future of sales and marketing.

To really see the shape and direction of technological change, we must appreciate the innumerable ways in which economic cycles, financial markets, extingencies of competition, regulatory extremes from Washington, the political climate in mid-America, and popular trends in social taste and spending all affect the long-term implementation and beneficial economic effects from the commercialization of new technologies.[4]

6

The largest deposit of copper in the world is now buried in New York City. Some 28,000 new cellular telephone subscribers are activated every day in the United States. Technology in general is changing so fast that we can hardly make sense of it all. The essentially revolutionary nature of the forces unleashed by the new technologies is indisputable. Little doubt exists that the digital revolution will change the way knowledge is gained and the way wealth is created. But, let's face it, in spite of these technical marvels, computers are still ridiculously unfriendly and the Web is absurdly awkward.

Some of the digital revolution's most noted thinkers argue that the world is now nearly a blank slate for the first time in centuries, and that digital bits and bytes are the electronic chisels for sculpting an entirely new world order. I disagree. Most people who promote and aggrandize technology choose, often knowingly, to ignore the burden of the tremendous infrastructure and amount of money invested in what these neothinkers would call "legacy technology."

Getting from here to there will be neither as easy nor as cheap as is too often suggested. Most of the technically savvy world is perpetually searching for the holy grail of the "killer application," resulting in companies trying to spin gold out of the cybersphere and it is gold that they often produce; though they often end up simply with a gold-paved cowpath.

In reality, very few technologies can exist right where the rubber hits the road. The applied technologies of telecommunications belong to that rare breed of endeavor where the technology of the future is juxtaposed with the reality of now. Coupled with the fact that, for all practical purposes, the 20th century was yesterday, this becomes even more dramatic. Therefore, if you want to go where the action is; if you wish to find an industry where you can readily embrace the locus of where you have moved – beyond substituting activity for achievement – I suggest that you look to the technologies of customer contact. The

7

technologies that have grown up over the last 25 years around the automatic call distributor are among the few disciplines where the pragmatic and profitable implementation of technology indisputably occurs.

So, somewhere between the utilitarian, proven "legacy" technologies such as the public branch exchange, and the seemingly unearthly, glittering cyberdomain of trillion bit-per-second transport, lies a middle ground... a path of least resistance that, if followed, will provide some assurance that those who don't stray too far afield can avoid speed wobble on the information superhighway. Stability lies ahead on the communications superhighway, but you must be able to judge which lane will get you there, which exits to take, and when to pause to refuel. This work is my attempt to render a roadside map of the specific technologies of the call center – specifically the technologies of customer contact.

The big picture can be narrowed down to something pretty small, and while digital technology may function at the speed of light, its fullest impact upon our social and economic lives will be felt only over time. History offers valuable lessons to those who may be tempted to believe that the final fruits and consequences of human endeavors can be predicted with any certainty.[5]

My advice? Don't take my word for it. This book is not a forecast but a quasi-technical commentary of our times. Develop your own vision, for I will certainly be wrong. Whatever the other technology pundits and I may say, ". . . have a vision for what the future will look like; and execute against that vision."[6]

If you want to take my advice about what to expect from the technologies of customer contact over the next five years, strike a balance between the progressive leader (the one running out in front of the pack yelling, "Follow me!") and the laggard (the one standing in the back yelling, "Charge!"). What the business manager needs to do until after the turn of the century is play the difference, avoiding the unprofitable creep of obsolescence while maintaining the existing infrastructure to support the tremendous base of consumers out there who still lead, and will continue to lead for some time, analog lives. Look to the companies that no longer think of themselves as telecommunication vendors or computer companies but as solutions providers, who execute and accomplish above technology.

---

[1]Kelly, K. (1994). *Out of Control: The Rise of the Neo-Biological Civilization.* Reading, MA: Addison-Wesley, 36.
[2]Burstein, D. (1995). *Road Warriors.* New York, NY, Dutton-Penquin Books, 351.
[3]Burstein, D. (1995). *Road Warriors.* New York, NY, Dutton-Penquin Books, 366.
[4]Burstein, D. (1995). *Road Warriors.* New York, NY, Dutton-Penquin Books, 6.
[5]Unknown, apologetic credit is given.
[6]Severino, P. (1996, April 8). *Forbes* ASAP, pp.103.

THE CENTER OF IT ALL

You can observe a lot just by watching.
– Yogi Berra

The digital revolution is the first technological shift in the epochs of human history to be observed in real time. And as an epoch-changing result, the digital revolution itself has become, in effect, aware. This awareness exists above technology and has manifested itself in many forms, but all have led to the wholesale reordering of the genetic makeup of our economies, political systems, social structures, and most importantly, our business cultures.

This revolution is driven by an incomprehensibly huge economy that zaps electronically, from one place to another, more than $2 trillion per day (60,000 years before the birth of Christ if each second were a dollar). Much is at stake, but most of the big money will be made on the outcome of how technology is used to transfer and communicate these trillions of bits of currency and information.

Building the telecommunications infrastructure for knowledge-based industries like banking, health care, and transportation represents the greatest potential for economic growth ever seen. Customer premises equipment providers, long-distance companies, Regional Bell Operating Companies (RBOCs), cellular phone companies, alternative access providers, Personal Communications Services providers, cable companies, and broadcast networks – everyone in the telecommunications business – is embroiled in a slugfest over control of an existing market that in 1995 had $300 billion a year in revenues.[1]

This book is written for those responsible for and involved in the storage, manipulation, and transmission of information and not in the creation of knowledge. Albeit a simplification, think carrier not content. Not that content isn't, in and of itself, a tremendous industry. You must keep in perspective the preeminence of Microsoft when you consider that Microsoft makes only half the revenues in a year that a company like Sony makes in a single quarter.

Digital communication: it's fast, cheap, interactive, and controlled by decentralized users. The new machines of today are between man and man (call centers) rather than between man and nature (trains). Relations and relationships are processed in these machines.

In the future, vast networks of wireless data, directed by powerful computers and intelligent machines, seem poised to transform the consumption experience, bringing some of the same efficiencies to the service sector that have already been capitalized on in manufacturing.

A Great Read for the Applications Manager

By the year 2002, roughly one half of all corporate high-tech spending will be devoted to intercompany connections, up from less than five percent today. Jerry Stead, former head of AT&T Global Information Solutions, said, "The collection, dissemination and analysis of customer information has become an essential prerequisite of a modern operation. Technology is no longer just an aid to the strategy – it is the heart of the strategy."[2]

Predictions call for companies to organize around "value streams" that will help get services to their customers faster. Future professionals in information technology will marry their technological know-how with an understanding of the value streams in their businesses. Every corporation has at least one strategic value stream; focusing on only one or two of the most important will be a key to corporate success. These streams are analogous to an application or, more specifically, a work-flow application – something above the level of technology. A consequence of this "value streaming" is the emerging requirement for a new type of business manager – an applications manager.

This book is written specifically for those managers and executives who are committed to using information technology to help their business consistently gain competitive advantages. For the last several decades, information services, computer technology, and telecommunications requirements have been a substantial part of every company's products and business processes. The difference today is that more and more senior executives are striving to understand technology and to learn how it can be applied to their companies. Yet, pleas to senior management within the adminisphere that the technology of customer contact is becoming critical to the growth of the company still fall too often on deaf ears. Why?

The biggest challenge facing call center and contact technology managers today is learning to speak the language of senior management and understanding how to communicate the call center's role, goals, and needs. A derivative of this challenge is insufficient resources, namely people, which adds to the inability to communicate effectively with top management.

Call centers have been managed typically at a service level, which means nothing to the president of the company. Call center managers (and technology managers in general) need to talk to senior management about finance; they need to talk about the trade-offs where the company has lost revenues because poor contact technology has turned customers away. They need to talk to the president about those customers who have taken their business elsewhere because they have been put on hold for too long or too often, and about the impact of poor service on the stockholders.

Instead, contact technology managers tend to talk about the average speed to answer, average hold time, the benefits of screen popping, and computer telephony integration (CTI). This is a manager training issue in a world where the company works hard at training agents and the managers who manage them, but very little effort is made to train managers to speak the language of the executive suite.

The technology managers are not always at fault here. Often the senior executives have not cared. Their perspective in the past has been that call centers, telephony, and telecommunications have been another of those necessary, evil departments — a budget burden. Call centers are often assumed to be simple operations because they revolve around the telephone. Because telephones are common objects in our culture, their familiarity makes it easy to underestimate complex management tasks involved in call center operations. In the past, this attitude has manifested most dramatically as upgrade obstruction.

No longer can the call center and telecommunications be considered the orphans of the organization. Senior managers are recognizing now that call centers are more than just a place to flush money — they are a real part of the total access of the company. The company call center, wherever it may reside, is no longer just a customer-service opportunity; it is a stakeholder handshake at your company's front door. Realize that many customers may never talk to anyone in the company other than the personnel in your call center.

Top managers are finally beginning to get it. They are looking now for managers in the call center to bring them the right information with which to make decisions. I expect that senior management will become more and more involved in the call center operations in the coming years.

Interestingly, when I looked at executive attitudes toward contact technology, it was the World Wide Web (WWW), as a form of automatic call distribution (ACD) bypass, that enlightened executives to the way companies

14

really communicate with their stakeholders. The realization by senior managers is that, as a high-consequence activity, if you do not know what you are doing, the damn thing will explode. The company call center is becoming the most important node on the corporate network as it handles such complex transactions such as voice, e-mail, fax, Internet, WWW, and image.

The applications and process manager now has an opportunity to gain more visibility for what is really going on with callers. Decisions for purchasing contact technology products are shifting to information systems executives and are considered a crucial part of the total technology plan.

Enter a new breed of telecommunications manager – manager of applications above the level of core technology. These new technology information managers are looking for data communications, networking solutions, and products. No longer will the traditional purchasing processes of the last 15 years work, where the telecommunications department was relatively independent in its selection, purchase, and implementation of call processing systems (PBX [private branch exchange], voice mail, interactive voice response, and so on).

These two skill sets are rarely possessed by the same individual or, even more rarely, found in the same department. The call center manager, the person who manages the business, has got to be in control of both in relationship to their applications. He or she is the business manager, and the business manager should be driving the technology, not the other way around.

Telecommunications managers have long said that up until now part of the communication problem (with management and stakeholders) was that you could not accomplish anything until you overcame the obstacles of technology. What do they do now — now that they no longer have those excuses?

So the call center manager and the business manager who read this can ask, "How soon do I have to start understanding these technologies, and do

I need to be a person capable of making purchasing decisions of technology?" Absolutely. What I am describing here is a migration of telecommunications specialists and experts toward the middle, into the realm of data and networks. If you are considered a specialist, you must be able to apply your knowledge widely. Otherwise, you will specialize yourself into obsolescence. You must decide whether to have breadth or depth.

The new information-driven economy has most executives, technologists, and vision-responsible managers recognizing that, just as control of natural resources and manufacturing capacity drove the creation of wealth during the Industrial Revolution, today it is the resources of knowledge, skill, and talent for contact technology.

About This Book

I have attempted here to provide a comprehensive argument that the focus of telecommunications technology is shifting to those departments in an organization that are responsible for strategic long-term planning and implementation of technology. Unlike in the past, when the primary telecommunications contact point was often just the telecommunications manager, this book is intended specifically to provide a strategic floor plan for discussion with senior executives who are responsible for determining the integrated role that the technology of customer contact, specifically call centers, will play in their corporate technology of the future. This is a strategic business forecast, incorporating and integrating the experience, opinions, and judgments of many call center and numerous non-call center professionals.

This book has two halves. The first discusses four broad driving forces affecting the evolution of the technology of customer contact. Although I certainly would agree that many others exist, I chose these four because they are the most influential and are traditionally not often considered in strategic thinking about contact technology: the economy, the device, the work force, and customer-intimate marketing. The second half of the book is a forecast made up of the narrow band of now, the broad band of tomorrow, and the middle band in between.

I do not describe technical subjects such as skills-based routing, average speed to answer, or fancy, real time management reports. Rather this book looks at how the call center fits into the big paradigmatic shift occurring outside of the traditional cloistered world of our respective disciplines. The discussion begins at the widest mouth of a world-view funnel, the global economy, and narrows down to a locus, a focal point called the call center. Although this book does not start discussing by call centers, it certainly ends up there.

To understand what is happening, look outside the world of call center technology. Look at the world of marketing, microprocessors, the economy, the Internet, and all of the other fast-paced changes taking place. With the use of anecdotal analysis, my mission here is to provide a forecast of technology and trends for those technology managers whose responsibilities include the delivery of networked computing infrastructure and distributed telephony applications.

This book is about new technology and the automation it produces. Automation itself has two massive and obvious trends: the push of technology and the pull of customer requirements. The pull side of the digital revolution comes from the consumers of technology and is driven by business trends. The push comes from vendors who constantly develop new product innovations, feature capabilities, and functions. This book is written for both.

Bits of the Economy

How has digitization affected the metabolism of the economy? In 10 to 15 years, given the advances in media and communication technology, you will be exchanging unimaginably immense volumes of information, in real time, with every individual stakeholder in your enterprise. Computers are not just used on the company side of the exchange but, increasingly, on the customer side as well.

Communication technology will soon connect us all through the real-time transmission of image, sound, and data; the rapid advances in technology enable us to locate and access stored information anywhere. Powerful computational abilities will be used to create ever more accurate simulations of reality and human interactions with machines.

In an era when traditional manufacturing and natural resource-based industries are declining, the service sector in the United States has successfully staked a claim in a new economy based on knowledge, information, and technology. The most visible evidence of this burgeoning service economy's grasp of the new information and knowledge-based economies of the next five years and beyond is the proliferation of call centers in North America.[3]

Over the next 10 years, every company will change the way it conducts its business. This process has been discussed for years and has garnered its own ubiquitous term: business re-engineering. The bottom line is that business re-engineering democratizes information within an organization. Successful companies are developing knowledge-based hierarchies where rank commands less than knowledge. The truly networked organization will gain power by giving it away. In their seminal book, *Re-Engineering the Corporation,* Hammer and Champy define re-engineering as a fundamental rethinking and radical redesign of business processes to achieve dramatic improvements in critical, contemporary measures of performance such as cost, quality, service, and speed. The authors perceive technology as the tool that permits this kind of re-engineering. I believe that the technologies found in call centers most fit the apex of this fundamental re-engineering.

Indicative of the isolation and nonintegration of telecommunications into the mainstream of most corporate information processes is that many, if not most, call center managers have never read *Re-Engineering the*

Corporation. I don't know of a single Chief Information Officer, Manager of Information Systems, or information technologist who has not.

The trends are only going to accelerate. For example, buying goods and services on-line is immature, but if even two percent of the annual $2 trillion in consumer retail spending could be captured on-line, it would be a $40 billion economy. Should a mass migration to home shopping materialize, consumers would redirect their orders to home shopping networks. Shipments would go out United Parcel Service or Federal Express (with Internet delivery status and specific scheduled delivery times). Customer billing would be handled by credit or debit card. Digital technology would give consumers more choice and buying power. The compounding effects of far more efficient buying and selling processes could be enormous.

The technology of this re-engineering has been decided: client/server applications will permit people to collaborate with one another, to share knowledge and expertise while unbounded by distance, language, or time zones. These electronic communication tools of technology, including all of the technologies of voice, are rapidly creating new types of work patterns and replacing traditional types. The new world order of developing digital communications contains the seamless integration of static media such as data, text, and still images (fax) as well as time-based media such as audio, voice, sound, and video.

The Device

Much has been invested in understanding what the most common consumer communication device will be after the turn of the century. The cable providers want you to use televisions, the personal computer manufacturers want you to think PCs, some believe in the screen phone, and even fewer believe in Personal Digital Assistants (PDAs). Internet-on-a-chip processors, cable modems, and digital broadcast satellite technology will soon bring unlimited bandwidth into our homes. In 1995, PCs outsold color TVs, the number of e-mail messages surpassed snail mail, and RBOC data traffic exceeded voice traffic.

Some analysts predict that by the year 2000, as many as 23 percent of U.S. households will have "smart" phones. Smart phones combine the capabilities of the PC with the familiarity of the touch-tone phone. Analysts on the advanced edge of pioneer thinking say that you cannot avoid this stuff. Companies will have to recognize that some customers are simply going to choose to do business with them over the Internet while others will remain mail-only customers.

Whatever the device, and it will certainly not be just one, its design will be governed by forces far greater than the inventiveness of any single manufacturer. Influences will come from many disciplines and will incorporate many theories. An example is the Negroponte Switch. This idea, that Nicholas Negroponte introduced in a meeting with George Gilder and telecommunications leader Northern Telecom, predicts that, in the future, all of the information coming through the ground in the form of wires will come through the air, or wirelessly, and that what comes through the air will be delivered through the ground. The bandwidth in the ground is infinite, while the bandwidth of the air is not. We have but one ether, and an unlimited capacity of fiber. The spectrum in the air, no matter how cleverly we use it, will become rarer and rarer. Within a short decade or two, the air spectrum will be used for communication with moving objects that cannot be tethered like planes, boats, cars, briefcases and wristwatches.[4]

As I wrote this book, President Clinton signed a directive expanding the government's satellite navigation and communications systems to airlines, automakers, and other businesses. A Rand Corporation study suggested that this could lead to a new $8.5 billion-a-year industry, essentially overnight.

But some, like GTE Chairman Charles Lee, say that certainly the world is changing, but not as fast as you would think from the predictions of the overheated pundits. Fiber optic cables became available in the late 1970s but did not become a viable investment until many years later. Consumers need a chance to catch up. The information highway is coming, but paving it will take a long time.

Does technology in the form of e-mail, voice mail, fax, on-line services, work groups, and videoconferencing threaten the lowly telephone wire? No. The telephone will continue to play a dominant role in most customer – and stakeholder – relations.

Who's Calling and Why?

Companies are beginning to realize that call centers are not just for customers. Help desks certainly require sophisticated contact management but increasingly so do shareholders, vendors, employees, and distributors. All these callers can be summed up in the term "stakeholder." A stakeholder is any group or person who has an interest, or stake, in a company's actions – not merely owners (who are often called shareholders) or customers.[5]

These stakeholders are demanding better service, faster solutions to problems, and higher quality products and services. Although stakeholder/customer contacts must be efficient, they must also meet standards of quality and effectiveness as defined by the stakeholder/customer. The truly empowered agents will have the information at their fingertips to provide the answers and guidance from their business systems to help make good decisions about contacts in progress, and the authority to satisfy customer demands.

Not all contacts are necessarily single-objective calls, nor do they come consistently from the same media. Often they develop into a multistage transaction involving not only the telephone but mail, the fax, or even the Internet. You need a real conglomeration of capabilities that are not identical every step of the way — calls are no longer homogenous. The bottom line is providing whatever kind of assistance your stakeholders need to get things done faster.

21

Who's Answering?

A call center is defined as a business that brings together three elements: phone circuits, a switching system, and people. The center is a place where any call can be answered by any agent. At least, that used to be the definition. Today's definition must include integration of available telephone and computer technologies to provide what callers and agents need, when they need it. What they need, when they want it, being delivered through the exponentially growing power of client/server-based architectures.

Because the world changes every day, you must stay on top of these technologies; but, while technology is fascinating, it is merely a tool. Technology alone does not and cannot provide answers or satisfying interactions between customers and company.

A harmonic convergence takes place among computers, communications, and market opportunities. An enormous infrastructure exists to build or deliver microprocessors, PCs, software, communications equipment, and high bandwidth devices. Broadband Asynchronous Transfer Mode (ATM) can and will change the economics of the Internet by providing leverage on the Internet through its 100 million-plus installed base of connected PCs and by using high-resolution graphics, surround-sound full-spectrum audio, and full-motion video – all on demand across networks.[6]

This is the world of the magnified message. Instead of being phone-centric, we shall be communication-centric, exploring applications such as e-mail, voice mail, groupware, project management, scheduling, and on-line records and files. We shall look at scenarios that integrate all or some of these applications and demonstrate their role in an enterprise's work flow.

Call Center Forecast

Casey Stengel said, "Forecasting is difficult, especially about the future."

Over the years, call center vendors have engaged in a feature war. First it was the shortest available routing over uniform call distribution. For a while it was Integrated Services Digital Network (ISDN), then it was Automatic Number Identification (ANI), and then, skills-based routing. Although we have gone from POTS to PANS[7], (Plain Old Telephone Service to Pretty Amazing New Stuff) in just a few short years, and in spite of the eminence of the Internet, most of us agree that people are still going to turn to their phones for interaction and service.

Because speeds on the information superhighway are only going to become higher, call centers become an important point of customer service for both small and large businesses. Orders for telecommunications gear, in one significant telecommunications equipment vendor's case, rose 31 percent to $2.64 billion, reflecting a higher and growing demand in North American markets.

In 1995, office communications revenue, which includes call center technology, increased 32 percent to $828 million. A strong demand exists, also, for wireless and high-speed fiber-optic network equipment. Newer emerging product offerings include Internet access, video transmission, and multimedia applications.

The vast bulk of the growth in the call center markets rests in small and medium-sized call centers becoming larger – not in large call centers getting bigger. These growing call centers are automating at an unprecedented rate. This explosive growth is accelerating on a chart at a 20-degree angle. The number of call centers themselves is growing, on average, at 15 percent per year.

I project that the growth for 400-line and above stand-alone call centers will be flat and will eventually decline. The increasing decentralization and fragmentation of businesses and markets engendered by new technologies only means that the big and the dumb will die much faster, and the small and the nimble will be able to seize opportunities more quickly.

Domestic growth for those call centers in the range of 75 to 400 agents is weak. Most of the call center growth is occurring in departments ranging from 1 to 75 agents. Help desk software for departments of this size is booming. The call center will soon be able to deliver the service capability with a down-sized call center server on a card.

Until several years ago, small customer service accounting departments, billing departments, and small sales operations were not perceived of as types of environments for ACDs. However, re-engineering has created operations that are taking on call center-type roles for the first time. The market growth starts at this departmental level. Departments with 10 people are growing to 20, 50, and then 100, and the call center function grows.

In many ways, this type of "seeded" growth is forcing call center technology vendors to design systems for these smaller sizes because if they do not get those customers when they are small, they will have no chance at them when they get big. Many departmental call centers have grown from very small to very large with outrageous rapidity.

The dynamic growth in this segment explains why the PBX vendors have been so successful in this market and will remain so for some time. They can provide a modularity and scalability throughout an organization, for every department or section, some of which may require call center functions. The PBX vendors are designing systems for this market that needs a phone system anyway and can benefit from call center technology.

In the short term, smaller companies and departments will turn to ISDN to accommodate their need for bandwidth, while larger companies will use frame relay. The long-term migration moves toward switched ATM networks.

Conclusion

Information technology is just beginning to stimulate the most powerful tsunami of economic growth in human history.[8] But beware of falling into the Gilder-cosm. George Gilder is a popular visionary technologist. His ideas regard an impending "tidal wave of bandwidth" at both consumer and enterprise levels and its potential impact on the market are, at the level of a call center technology, a trifle overstated.

Unquestionably, the telecommunications infrastructure demanded of call centers has grown into a huge arena with many significant facets, all influencing the digital landscape. Policy reform, access, standards, advanced R&D, privacy, piracy, international economic competitiveness, and many more are still cloudy issues of public concern.

The information superhighway envisioned in the early 1990s – interconnected broadband networks delivering everything from wireless e-mail to interactive TV and full-motion video call centers – has been delayed considerably by the reality of the technology and its high costs. The day of digital reckoning with electronic delivery may be further off than we think for both economic and cultural, but not technical, reasons.

Clearly the client/server information-sharing architecture will be the supporting environment in which most of these structural changes will take place. Voice will be a required element, relegated perhaps as the most underestimated and least glamorous component in the business technology of the future but, nevertheless, a substantial part of the enterprise picture.

Voice, or the telephone, will always be the most accessible media. However, as a part of the total multimedia package of the future, voice will evolve and be accessed not only from the phone but from other devices such as the smart phone, the PC, or the universal mailbox on the desktop. The richness of mixed-media messaging will redefine the way people come together to add value to an enterprise.

For product-leadership companies, the toughest challenge is to envision the next technology, the next concept that lies beyond the bounds of their expertise. For the customer-intimate companies, the toughest challenge is letting go of current solutions and old technologies and moving themselves and their clients to the next paradigm.[9]

These technology tools address specifically flattening of the organization, moving of information horizontally rather than vertically to hierarchies, and establishing teams, both real and virtual. These teams can reach across organizations, across locations, or across the world. The virtual corporation of the 21st century will have its center in one place, the technology of customer contact.

Keeping track of four trends and one technology can give you a good compass, pointing the direction in which the digital winds are blowing. The technology is client/server and the four trends include the economy, the device, the agents, and the future of one-to-one marketing.

---

[1]Burstein, D. (1995). *Road Warriors.* New York, NY, Dutton-Penquin, 349.
[2]Tapscott, D. (1994). *The Digital Economy.* New York, NY McGraw-Hill, 5.
[3]Delottinville, P. (1994). *Shifting to the New Economy, Call Centers and Beyond.* Toronto, Canada, Copp-Clark, 5.
[4]Negroponte, N. (1995). *Being Digital.* New York, NY, Knopf, 1995, 24.
[5]This term came into frequent use by Tony Blair, a British dignitary, as described in a William Safire column.
[6]Kessler, A. (1996, Feb. 26). "Go Ahead—Jump!," *Forbes ASAP,* 45.
[7]Shafer, P. (1996). Pat introduced this phrase in several presentations and conversations.
[8]Heilemann,J. (1996, March). "It's the New Economy Stupid!" *Wired Magazine,*180.
[9]Treacy, and Wiersema. (1995). *The Discipline of Market Leaders.* Reading, MA, Addison Wesley, 191.

THE DIGITAL ECONOMY

It's All Ones and Zeros, from Atoms to Bits[1]

Martha Rogers, author of *The One to One Future,* opened a presentation with this astounding fact: in 1980, the largest deposit of copper in the world was located in the country of Chile; by 1995, it was in New York City. New York City alone has more than six million telephones, more phones than are in the entire country of Spain. Manhattan has more telephone lines than does the entire sub-Sahara Africa. The cables serving New York City have more than 33 million miles of copper wire.

The Pentagon in Arlington, Virginia has more than 568,000 miles of telephone lines. Washington, D.C. contains more telephones than people. More than 300 million telephone calls will be completed every hour by the year 2000. Over the next 15 years, 800 million new phone lines are expected to be installed worldwide, and more than 1.3 billion wireless phones will be deployed. Some 94 percent of U.S. households have telephones. Almost all have radios and television. Two-thirds have video cassette recorders and more than three-fifths have cable television. About one-quarter of all U.S. households have a personal computer.[2]

The transformation of the new economy has accelerated at a mind-bending speed. From Bill Gates and Microsoft to the Internet and on-line with the Web, from derivatives and fractual finance to Turbo Tax and e-mail, the abstractions and character of the new world's digital order have been assimilated into our lives to an extent that would have been unimaginable even in the late 1980s.

In the new economy, the means of production comes increasingly from the minds of the producers. Knowledge now produces wealth. Microsoft has created an estimated 1,200 millionaires among the company's employees, all who held early stock positions. The key assets of most companies are shifting from cash reserves and physical plants to the resources of intellectual skill, knowledge, and information.

Digital technology does, indeed, tend to blur the old boundaries between industries and markets by distilling the content of our communications, entertainment, media, and publishing into their common elements – digital ones and zeros – and then alchemizing them into incredible new economic possibilities. One reason that all media have become digital so quickly is that we have achieved very high levels of compression much sooner than most people predicted.

Before the end of the decade, the cost of installing and maintaining optical fiber, foot for foot, will be lower than the cost of installing and maintaining traditional "twisted pair" copper phone wire. Old analog lines have been replaced by digital switching, providing better and cheaper service.

Proponents (some are still out there) of the analog circuit are, themselves, hopelessly analog, as in "anal-log." Being "anal-log" describes those who refuse hopelessly to buy into the inevitable digital-ness of everything.

Economic History

Can you remember life before World Wide Web sites? Amazingly, we still live in a generation when not everyone in America has a phone; seven million American homes have no basic telephone service. Equally telling is that in some of America's ghetto communities, the penetration of cable TV is actually higher than that of telephones. What kind of economic impact could this possibly have on me if I influence technology decisions in my enterprise?

If your customers live in a ghetto, you had better to learn to talk to them through their televisions. It is doubtful that even America will ever become a nation in which everyone has computers, intelligent TVs, modems, network services, on-line service accounts, or any other on-ramp to the information superhighway.

Still, seven million U.S. homes without telephones represent less than 2 percent of the U.S. population and are insignificant compared to the overall growth in billions of dollars invested in customer services. The service sector now accounts for more than 70 percent of all jobs and output in the United States, while manufacturing as an economic sector is declining in its impact on the U.S. economy and has stabilized at approximately 20 percent of the American work force.[3]

We are at the upturn of a 100-year shift, transforming ourselves from an industrial-based economy dependent on land, labor, and capital into a knowledge-based economy based on information. Is the value of Intel in its plants, machines, robots, and real estate? Is the value of 3M in its huge warehouses holding billions of Post-it Notes? No, these companies' values lies in their distribution, patents, people, and processes. Rapid advances in telecommunications technology are creating whole new industries and services dedicated to satisfying the modern world's insatiable appetite for information.

Power has shifted from natural resources to knowledge resources; knowledge has become the key raw material for creating economic wealth. Information has become currency. Information is an economic asset. The revolution in information and communications technology has made knowledge the new competitive resource.[4]

Like a piece of capital equipment, a factory, or a patent, individual customer information has the capacity to improve a firm's productivity and reduce its costs. As with any other asset, this kind of information is not obtained without price. It is a valuable commodity that must be protected, nurtured, and developed. Used properly, this asset can yield a return for decades.[5]

And while the global economy is still driven by manufacturing-based industries, a dominant portion of the U.S. economy is shifting even more toward information-intensive service industries. This shift is leading to a greater demand for high-tech telecommunications platforms, systems, and services. We are going from brawn to brainpower, from manufacturing to service, and from mainframe to microprocessor. Heavy industries that were once vertically integrated under hierarchical management now look more like decentralized high-technology industries with horizontal matrices of virtual organizations.

The industrial machine age involved hierarchies, moving assembly lines, big companies, big unions, big cities, and big government. The thrust of this new economy is more Jeffersonian, empowering individuals to act, regardless of a physical presence. And we are just at the Model T stage of it.[6]

Speaking of cars, more Americans build computers than cars, more make semiconductors than construction machinery, more work in data processing than in petroleum refining. Since 1990, U.S. firms have spent more on computers and communications gear than on all other capital equipment combined. Software is the country's fastest growing industry. World trade in information-related goods and services is growing five times faster than trade in natural resources.[7]

Since 1991, U.S. investment in the basic tools of the information age, including computers and telecommunications equipment, has outpaced capital spending for heavy industrial hardware. By 1992, only one year after the two trend lines had crossed for the first time, capital investment in information technology and telecommunications gear was nearly $25 billion higher than the traditional industrial capital investment, and pulling away fast.[8] This economic fact alone supports the rising trend behind the purchase and high-tech reconditioning of old factory space in the United States.

According to the U.S. Chamber of Commerce, business and consumer spending on information technology has accounted for 36 percent of economic growth since 1990. The United States is also running a huge ($3 billion) trade surplus in computer-related services.[9] Worldwide, trade is growing five times more quickly in knowledge-related goods and services than in other resources. In 1995, information technology excluding content in Canada was almost a $50 billion industry and accounted for more than 6 percent of the Gross Domestic Product. The software industry accounts for 21 percent of all R&D in Canada.[10]

The pace of this pulling away is driven in the real world by Moore's law. Named after one of the digital founding fathers, Moore's law says that roughly every 18 months, the computational power of computers doubles. In the wacky, unpredictable domain of digits, bits, and bytes, this is one of the few axioms reliably standing the test of time (digital time, that is, not analog).

Every 20 years since 1900, the amount of computational power — machine brainpower — that can be bought with one dollar has increased by a factor of a thousand. That is more than a millionfold increase just since 1950. We are in a period now when cycles move by months, not years. This is the same evolution that makes Genesis's 32 bit, 200 million instructions per second (MIPS) game computer more powerful than a multimillion dollar 1976 Cray supercomputer. As recently as five years ago, this processing speed would have cost as much as a $2 million mainframe.

Those who even talk about national economies and their relative competitiveness are living in an ancient time warp, failing to get with the program of a new global village whose marketplace is linked by seamless telecommunications networks. Today we can track the individual purchases and transactions of millions of individual global customers simultaneously for the same cost required to track a few hundred customers in 1970. Advances in computer and communication technology now put a share-of-customers approach within reach of virtually every business in the world.

Although fantastic returns are being made on the content side of the digital economy, making movies instead of sending them, it is the transmission side of the equation, our digital infrastructure, that supports it all. Telecommunications is the Hercules of the digital domain.

In the past two years, spending on everything from modems to high-speed digital switches has soared by 53 percent, to almost $100 billion, double the rate of spending growth in computers and other capital equipment. "This is a great time to be a supplier," said John Roth, Northern Telecom's North American president. "Everybody out there is doing a lot of planning in infrastructure."[11]

Depending on which digital business you are talking about, growth rates vary consistently between 3 percent and 10 percent faster than the rest of the economy. Worldwide, the PBX market reached an all-time high of $20 billion in 1994; $6.5 billion of that was in the United States alone. In 1995, U.S. telecommunications industry earnings alone grew more than 15 percent to $6.8 billion. Telephony is one of the world's highest-growth businesses.

Growth was healthy in core markets: data communications (19 percent), call processing (15 percent), and PBXs (6 percent). Emerging markets saw even more dramatic growth: wireless office hardware (100 percent), computer telephony integration (44 percent), and teleconferencing (41 percent).[12] Some disciplines, such as call center and PBX technologies, are off the charts for established companies such as Nortel and Lucent.

In the United States, roughly 100,000 call centers have been established. Dataquest estimates that American businesses will buy and implement between 8,000 and 10,000 new ACD systems in 1996 and 1997, respectively. In the mid-1970s, the price of an ACD position was about $10,000; today the price of a fully featured ACD position is less than $3,000. Long-distance charges used to be a major expense. In 1985, an 800-number circuit was priced at a flat $1,700 per month. In 1995, the cost was less than $30 per month.[13]

Merging, not emerging, technology characterizes the new economy. Computer telephony integration (CTI) is the closest thing we have to describing the convergence and hybridization of these technologies. The locus of this junction is most visibly the call center.

Caught between a $100 billion-a-year telecommunications industry and a $100 billion-a-year computer systems industry is this $5 billion-a-year CTI industry. The CTI industry reached $3.5 billion in sales in 1995 and is growing at 30 percent to 40 percent annually. Consulting and integration revenues from CTI are expected to exceed $8 billion by 1999 (source: Dataquest 4/95).

Because of the competition in the marketplace, the price of switches and computers will continue to drop while the quality and capacity of these switches and computers will continue to rise. Stable support from a global investment community will insure the availability of capital for long-term growth in telecommunications. In the next 10 years, companies around the world engaged in the development, manufacturing, or sale of telecommunications services, and specifically call center equipment and systems, will have access to plenty of capital.

Businesses have been eager buyers of the latest and greatest in high technology since the 1980s, spending billions on upgrades with each new generation of Intel chips and Microsoft software. But as the economic expansion ages, some companies are starting to shift technology dollars to meet other needs.

Getting value from cyberspace will relate only marginally to issues of cost and access. A much larger role will be played by knowledge, skill, and culture. Understanding the money potentially recoverable through investment in technology and the economics of where that recovery comes from is important.

The Stats about Who Will Be Calling

The desktop personal computer (PC) market exceeds $150 billion, and 1995 PC software and hardware sales alone totaled $116 billion. In addition, 70 percent of all businesses have a local area network (LAN) with network-based information environments. The number of orbiting communications satellites is expected to double, and the number of computers will more than double.

About 28,000 people within the United States sign up for cellular service every day.[14] The country contains 50 million computers. The satellite dishes, which sell for around $600, are having one of the highest adoption rates ever seen in consumer electronics. Since their introduction in mid-1993, a total of 2.5 million units have been sold and installed. In contrast to the ten years it took color TV manufacturers to sell 1 million TV sets, it took only four years to sell 1 million VCRs.

A single fiber-optic strand as thin as a human hair can carry thousands of times more information than a conventional copper wire. Most long-distance traffic is carried at one point or another via fiber optic. Developed in 1952, optic fibers were only able to carry light rays a few feet. Today they can carry, on average, 3.4 billion bits per second. Fiber optics are the backbone of emerging technologies such as digital switches and huge networks. Cellular phones and pagers are becoming the predominant electronic gateways that link computers, telephones, and on-line databases.

In 1946, for a phone call to be switched by operators and placed coast to coast took 96 seconds. Today computers connect us in fewer than 3 seconds. The universe of on-line databases in the 1960s numbered several dozen and had grown to 2,800 by 1984. By 1992, the number of databases had grown to more than 10,000.[15] And what are they doing? They are making calls, a lot of calls: phone calls, data calls, long distance calls, 800-number calls, and 900-number calls.

I can comfortably say that this phenomenon is only going to grow bigger. More than one half of the international world has never made a phone call.[16] To put our telephone "centric-ness" into proper perspective, compare the United States to the rest of the world. Only seven percent of the residents in Latin America and one percent of Asian and African residents have access to a phone.[17] With 2.5 million people on the list, the wait for a telephone in India is seven or eight years.[18]

More than three billion people in emerging economies around the world lack access to the basic telephone dial tone. China and the Indian subcontinent are home to almost half of the world's population, yet each has an average of fewer than 2 telephones per 100 people, in contrast to the United States, which has more than 50 phone lines per 100 people.[19] Vietnam has only has .025 phones per 100 people.

After all is said and done, we may find that these undeveloped nations' lack of infrastructure may have been a blessing in disguise as the United States strives to keep pace with countries unburdened by the weight of hundreds of millions of miles of plain old twisted pair copper wire. It is already much cheaper and easier to lay fiber from scratch for backbone networks or to utilize coaxial cables, satellites, and cellular technology than to string wire from pole to pole.[20] What we consider undeveloped, may turn out to have been just underestimated.

A harmonic convergence is taking place among computers, communications, customer service, and market opportunities. An enormous infrastructure exists to build or deliver microprocessors, PCs, software, communications equipment, and high-bandwidth communications. Opportunities abound to find ways to leverage the Internet and the 100 million-installed base of interconnected PCs, and to use high-resolution graphics, audio, and eventually video across networks.

Our Population of Customers

A fundamental question for both the producers and the consumers of this telecommunications gear asks where all our customers are going to come from and how they will call us. Technology is developed in response to trends in changing life-styles. Trends that favor people becoming more mobile, interactive, and connected favor multimedia messaging that includes video, voice, and data, so people can access them easily, regardless of time or geography.

The population of the United States is expected to reach 274.6 million in the year 2000, up from 256 million in 1995. The population for the year 2050 is expected to reach 394 million. This becomes relevant in determining digital literacy. Only the digitally literate would contact your company by e-mail or the Internet. The baby boomers are the most digitally informed segment of the population. This will be discussed in more detail in the next chapter, but one reason for the slower-than-expected decline of the telephone as a dominant communications device in our culture is best expressed in the adage, "You can't teach an old dog new tricks."

New population figures from the Census Bureau indicate that the baby boom is beginning to lose its long ascendancy as the nation's premier generation. As of 1996, baby boomers aged 32 to 50 years number 78 million and account for 29 percent of the population. By 2006, the number of boomers will drop to 76 million, at which point they will constitute only 26 percent of the population. The smaller, so-called Generation X-ers, born between 1965 and 1976, are currently aged 20 to 31 years but will not be able to claim ascendancy over the original boomers until sometime after 2030.[21]

And what do most of these 256 million people, you, and I have in common? We transact.

Banking and Financial Services

Digital communications networks move nearly $2 trillion a day globally, compared with only $1 trillion a year in physically traded goods.[22] Telecommunication serves as an electronic trade route for much of the world's commerce.

Today, capital flows across borders electronically, and transnational companies compete in multiple markets and time zones. Modern telecommunications technology offers businesses, governments, and organizations a valuable edge in this fiercely competitive market – e-cash, no paper work, and total anonymity. Being connected to the worldwide telecommunications network is as essential to a company's growth today as accesses to deep harbors, railroad spurs, or other strategic locations on trade routes were to pioneers in the past. Telecommunication offers invaluable access to information and markets, helping companies to overcome economic or geographic limitations as well as to compete effectively and attract foreign investment.

The development of many new technologies is driven by the complex communications needs of large service industries like financial services, health and medical care, retail sales, travel, and education. These industries are expanding broadly.

The United States spends almost 1.5 percent of its Gross Domestic Product each year to process payments through the banking system, and yet the European Common Market system is so sophisticated that it typically spends only one third as much as does the United States.

Without computers, the New York Stock Exchange would need 20,000 floor clerks to handle the half-billion shares exchanged daily.

The United States has 11,000 banks. (Amazingly, between 10 percent and 12 percent of all Americans are "unbanked"; that is, they have no account or relationship with a financial institution.) In 1995, a total of 61 billion checks were transacted. The average check amount was $1,000. Check-processing volume is growing annually at a rate of 2 percent to 3 percent. Any benefit from check floating has been eliminated because 90 percent of all checks are cleared the following business day.

Even if you are not computer literate, if you have used an automatic teller machine card, you have actually "surfed the Net." On-line services are accessed millions of times a day through personal computers. Millions of computers around the world talk to each other over the same phone lines we use for daily conversation.

Some 70 percent of all Americans have automatic teller machine cards.[23] Americans made almost nine billion ATM transactions in 1995 using 410,000 ATMs worldwide, 105,000 of which are in the United States. The Tyme network based ATM machines alone were used more than 72 million times in 1995, with each customer spending 30 seconds on an average withdrawal. Debit card use rose to 1.43 billion transactions, up 53 percent from 1994. These debit card figures do not include transactions performed at ATMs.[24] The reason banks love ATM machines but prefer for us, as consumers, not to know this is because they can charge a nominal fee, from $12 to $15 a month, for us to stay out of their lobbies and offices.

1997 will be the year that on-line banking will be placed on the map. While most customers have yet to experience full-service remote banking, many more will get their arms twisted in a fever of marketing for on-line banking. The benefits of cyberbanking are irrefutable and irreversible. Cyberbanks never close, you can take your account wherever you move, and no primitive stamp licking will be involved ever again.

The controlling drive behind electronic banking is that it offers a new way to build market presence without adding brick and mortar.

Currently, on-line banking requires a $50 program and a PC. With a modem, anyone can connect directly to his or her bank account to check balances on the screen in real time, transfer funds between accounts, and initiate payments to any vendor or creditor.

In 1995, some 720,000 of the 10.3 million households that were on-line in the United States made an on-line purchase (source: Inteco Corp).

Consumer Spending On-Line:

Past and projected dollars spent per year buying products offered on-line.

1994	1995	1996	1997	1998	1999	2000
0.24	0.35	0.52	0.95	2.30	4.50	6.90

Revenues in billions, in U.S. dollars (source: Forrester Research)

No living person appears to enter into the on-line purchasing equation. On the contrary. Call centers are sustaining entire on-line transaction based institutions. There are more than 57,000 call center related jobs in the banking industry alone. Most enterprises are migrating toward the generation of business activity over the telephone. Call centers are now opening accounts, completing transactions such as transfers, and tremendously lessening the burden on branches. Call centers are answering millions of calls per month for institutions of all sizes, and are preventing banks from spending additional money on branches and personnel.

Minneapolis-based Norwest Financial Services Corp. handles 1.2 million calls per month, up 152 percent since 1992. Norwest alone operates 10 call centers to support adequately that volume of calls. Like the automatic teller machines, telephones and voice-response units help automate routine banking events and lower staffing costs. Norwest estimates that it has generated 13,188 new loans for $73 million in less than two years. Of all banking customers, 68 percent bank through the voice-response unit, 24 percent bank mostly through the interactive voice response (IVR), 4 percent to 5 percent will ask for the operator, and 3 percent will abandon the call.[25]

Political Regulation

The wave of telecommunications deregulation that began in 1995 is just the start of a beachful of waves. The next wave will be the further elimination of additional government and legal barriers in cellular, computer, cable television, publishing, and other service and information-intensive industries.

The telecommunications market and industry need to be perfectly clear on the fact that free markets are far more effective at "protecting" the consumers of customer premises equipment (CPE) than are government controls. The benefits to consumers will depend on unbridled competition within the industry, and government intervention will only hinder its evolution.

Government cannot standardize efficiently an industry that changes practically by the minute. We must realize the importance of voluntary exchange and market forces in producing efficient results. Microsoft is a company with great potential to destroy the federal postal monopoly by promoting and developing the widespread use of electronic mail while being attacked simultaneously by a government agency created to break up monopolies. The market – not the government – should determine the winners and the losers.[26]

And what about the post office? The future of the post office is looking bleak as our business culture wakes up to the fact that everything that can be passed through the post office today can eventually pass through Web servers and Internet messaging-type devices at much lower prices and near-instantaneous speeds, with many new features for replying, indexing, saving, and carrying out transactions.[27]

While political and other uncertainties exist regarding some issues, the elimination of these barriers will create an explosion of new services, markets, and opportunities for call center technology. For example, look what has happened for telecommunications in the banking industry alone.

In his book *The Road Ahead,* Bill Gates writes about the information highway of the future creating Adam Smith's 200-year-old ideal system of perfectly competitive markets: consumers will be well informed and free to choose from the world's supply of goods and services, and computers will empower everyday people. Like Adam Smith before him, Bill Gates believes that capitalism is the best means to serve, protect, and accommodate the common man. He believes that the computer-linked world is the best means to achieve what he calls "friction free capitalism." It doesn't get any more friction free than the global network of seamless light-based information streaming.

Conclusion

The transformation from atoms to bits is irrevocable and unstoppable.[28]

Telecommunication demand is on the rise throughout the developing world, fueled by growing urbanization, increasing per capita income, and higher standards of living. These emerging markets will grow to a $1 trillion business over the next 20 years. Global telecommunication presents an excellent opportunity to capitalize on the growth in worldwide demand for information and the means in which it travels.

However, the emergence of a digitally based "friction free capitalism" will be anything but frictionless. The transition being wrought by chips and bits from the industrial age to the information age will be long and drawn out, typified by the lingering on of the telephone and the huge horde of digitally illiterate masses. This transformation will take many years.

The era of interactive (non-Internet based) multimedia on demand will arrive slowly and take seven or eight years (best-case scenario) to become established as a mass market phenomenon. The smart money, in many contexts, is in putting off these capital technology purchases for the desktop as long as possible. Instead of focusing on raw horsepower or which Windows operating systems to use, technologists should decide first what new business functions they want to perform and then shop for the technology to do them. The days of buying equipment and then searching around for applications are gone. Slowly disappearing are the days when you could buy hardware for ornaments.

In the background is this nagging, common notion that something big is changing in the conduct of capitalism. The real-world futurists see increasing globalization of national economies, with digital technologies playing a powerful role in accelerating that process. Most people jokingly slough off an appreciation that the economy is realizing an epochal change. Nevertheless, the computer's digital vocabulary of ones and zeros is becoming the common language of the entire economy.[29]

Customers are seeking increased accessibility to information – accessibility that is simple and easy and that bridges the gap between voice and data. Some advances in communications and, specifically, in call center technology may take years and more capital investment before they ever reach the marketplace.

Like most other economic processes, building the information highway will be a complex and expensive evolutionary process that will proceed on a crooked path. It took almost 70 fitful years to wire half of America for basic telephone service. We have settled culturally on the telephone as our predominant user interface of choice. It is certain now that the long anticipated convergence of voice, data, and video is picking up a head of steam.

The last economic and technical revolution took place in the United

States around 1840, when the train and the telegraph converged to form the first high-technology sector in the country. Within a decade, companies had to reorganize so they could operate in terms of minutes rather than days. Suddenly you could know the prices of goods in far-away markets and ship goods in a truly integrated market fashion.

The train and the telegraph, each alone, would not have changed the face of America. The train by itself would only have been a faster Pony Express. The telegraph would only have given people the ability to interact at a distance, without gaining a significant consequence from that interaction. When combined, however, the two created a new concept of distribution, producing a new type of market economy.

And precisely 150 years later, we can see in retrospect that the telegraph was only a precursor of the device that could probably be billed on the list of the top ten inventions that shaped the legacy of human culture: the telephone.

[1]Negroponte, N. (1995). *Being Digital.* New York, NY, Knopf, 36.
[2]Darden, P. [Online]. Available HTTP:\\www.ntia.doc.gov.
[3]Burstein, D. (1995). *Road Warriors.* New York, NY, Dutton-Penquin, 292.
[4]*Harvard Business Review,* "What's So New About the New Economy," unk. date.
[5]Burstein, D. (1995). *Road Warriors.* New York, NY, Dutton-Penquin, 240
[6]Forbes, S. (1996, March). [Interview]. *Wired Magazine,*180.
[7]Heilemann, J. (1996, March). "It's the New Economy, Stupid." *Wired Magazine,* 68.
[8]Burstein, D. (1995). *Road Warriors.* New York, NY, Dutton-Penquin, 274.
[9]Mandell, M. (1994). "The Digital Juggernaught." *Business Week,* 22.
[10]From Industry Canada Data.
[11]Arnst, C. (1996, April 8). "Special report: The Coming Telescramble." *Business Week,* 66.
[12]Source: "Multimedia Telecommunications Market Review and Forecast, BCR, pp 8, Mar 1996
[13]Durr, W. (1995). Building a World Class Call Center. Waterloo, IA, *Teleprofessional,* 5.
[14]Source: Cellular Telecommunications Industry Association, March 13, 1995.
[15]Burstein, D(1995). *Road Warriors.* New York, NY, Dutton-Penquin, 355.
[16]Nash, N. (1995, Feb. 27). "Group of Seven Defines Policies About Telecommunications." *New York Times,* A1.
[17](1994, Sept. 26). *Business Week,* 35.
[18](1994, Aug./Sept.). *Infrastructure Finance,* 16.
[19](1994, Oct.). Telegeography 1994. TeleGeography, Inc.

[20]Burstein, D. (1995). *Road Warriors.* New York, NY, Dutton-Penquin, 295.

[21]Crispell, D. (1996, March 25). "US Population Forecast Decline for 2000," *Journal of Am. Demographics,* 89.

[22]Stone, A. (1996, Feb. 14). "We Are in the Middle Age of Computers." *USA Today,* 1A.

[23]Nelson, R. (1996, March). "Brave New Electronic Transactions." *Popular Science,* 65.

[24](1996, March 27). Nielson Report. *Wall Street Journal,* B3.

[25]Bank Automation News, Presentation at the ABA Solutions Conference '96. via Indivuidual.

[26]Khalil, S. "Microsoft and the 'Invisible Hand.'" *Wall Street Journal,* B2. (1995). *Road Warriors.* New York, NY, Dutton-Penquin, 56.

[27](1994, May 9). Data On Job Eliminations. *Business Week,* 77.

[28]Negroponte, N. (1995). *Being Digital.* New York, NY, Knopf, 121.

[29]Burstein, D. (1995). *Road Warriors.* New York, NY, Dutton-Penquin, 177.

THE DEVICE

If you know your history, the future will not trouble you.
– African Proverb

A lot of money is riding (ringing?) on understanding what the universal communications appliance of the future will be. To build an efficient infrastructure of contact technology, you must know exactly how your customer will be calling you. Will it be still by phone, by PC, by TV, or by smart phone? How soon will we be using it? At what speed will the telephone decline as the principal device we use to communicate?

Contrary to the hype of many pundits, several compelling reasons explain why the simple telephone or some sophisticated derivative of it will remain the standard device for many years to come. Each reason by itself would be compelling enough to make the argument.

The most impressive explanation for the sustaining power of the analog telephone is found in an odd, cyclical coincidence of history. A 30-year evolutionary process appears to be at work here. If you look at the history of major, culture-changing communication devices over the past 150 years, you can see the pattern that emerges.[1]

1840	Telegraph...Morse
1876	Telephone...Bell
1901	Radio...Marconi
1929	Television...Sarnoff
1962	Mainframe Computers...IBM
1989	PC with Modems...Microsoft

If you know your history, the future will not be a problem.

Predicting the future technology of customer contact is rooted in the coincidence of this 30-year, periodic cycle. In its day, each invention has proved to be the most important advance in shaping our communicating culture. I start with the telegraph, as opposed to the Gutenberg Press, because it marks when we began using electrons instead of letters.

The — - . .-.. . —. .-. .- .—. ....

The first instrument to transform information into electrical form and transmit it reliably over long distances was the telegraph, developed by Samuel Morse in the 1840s. The telegraph ignited the slow fuse that has burned into today's information age.

"Morse Code," a dash-dot system that sends individual letters in a message, is still used today to transmit messages, mostly by short-wave radio. The original Morse telegraph did not use a key and sounder. It was a device designed to print patterns. Morse developed his first commercial telegraph with a key and sounder in 1846. Ironically, the telegram was discontinued by Western Union in December 1991, and the last wire-line telegraphed message was sent at the end of 1995, almost 150 years to the date of the first message transmitted by Morse.

The revolution that took place in the economy in 1840 as a result of the telegraph forced companies to restructure so they could manage in terms of minutes rather than days. Suddenly you could know the price and quantity of goods in distant markets and arrange to ship goods in a truly integrated, near real-time market fashion. Without the telegraph, the train alone would have been merely a faster Pony Express.

With the combination of the train and the telegraph, a new concept of distribution occurred, producing a new type of financial market: the technology futures market. Arriving at the station at the same time, the train and the telegraph "converged" in the 1840s to create the first high-tech sector in U.S. society. This convergence has been repeated through several generations and currently manifests itself in CTI.

The Telephone

What Alexander Graham Bell was really trying to invent when he developed the first crude telephone was a microphone for deaf people. In 1876, Bell created his "electrical speech machine," commonly called the first telephone. Bell had set up the first telephone exchange in Connecticut by 1878. By 1884, long-distance connections were made between Boston and New York City. And, as stated previously, by 1995 New York City contained more copper wiring than did the entire country of Chile.

The Radio

Guglielmo Marconi came up with the idea of using electromagnetic waves for long-distance communication around 100 years ago, in the 1890s. In 1895, he produced the first practical wireless telegraph system, and the first wireless message was sent across the English Channel in March 1899. The first transatlantic communication, which involved sending the Morse code signal for the letter "s," was sent on December 12, 1901, from England to Newfoundland. For the next 30 years, further advancement in radio was made possible by the development of the electron tube. The invention of the diode permitted the detection of high-frequency radio waves and the ability to amplify radio and sound waves. Now we have 28,000 new cellular subscribers per day.

Television

Thirty years later, in 1929, David Sarnoff invested $50 million in all-electronic television experiments. Sarnoff had demonstrated television at the 1939 New York World's Fair, and the company he started to support his invention eventually became RCA. Franklin D. Roosevelt spoke before the camera, becoming the first president to appear on television. The rapid development of television was delayed both by the war and by an early example of bureaucratic morass in a struggle over wavelength allocations and government regulation. Television was almost killed by government interest in FM radio. Little did we know then that 50 years later we would still be having billion dollar battles over the government's frequency spectrum allocations.

Computers

The integrated circuit, a tiny chip of silicone containing an entire electronic circuit, was invented in 1959. This invention led to development of small, rugged, efficient, and relatively inexpensive minicomputers. Unlike mainframes, these compact machines could be installed almost anywhere and used by almost anyone.

By the early 1960s, efforts to design and develop the fastest possible computers were well underway. The major computer manufacturers began to offer a range of computer capabilities and costs as well as various peripheral equipment. Manufacturers offered such things as consoles, card feeders, page printers, cathode-ray tube displays, graphing devices, and magnetic-disk file storage. These were used widely in businesses for such applications as accounting, payroll, inventory control, ordering supplies, and billing.

PCs with Modems

Almost exactly another thirty years later, PCs went from being used for word processing and spreadsheets to being used as communications devices. The PCs of 1990 held more computational power than the Apollo spacecrafts; this dramatic increase in processing power ushered in a decade characterized by BBSs, email, the Internet, and now the WWW. Today, PCs come with video cameras and sell for less than $1,000. Desktop computers have become telecommunications centers through which data, print, sound, and video can be transmitted easily throughout the world. We are entering a future in which the telephone, computer, fax, television, and mail will be linked together in a single or several networks accessed from and through banks of modems sitting in the chassis of most computers.

The Evolution

We see that evolutionary communication developments occur roughly every 30 years and, so far, have had 150-year life spans. Generational change occurs roughly every 30 years, in spite of the appearance that Moore's law and the incremental power of the microchip have driven the impression of generational change time spans down to years or maybe even months.

Note the compression occurring here. The speed at which we receive information is quickening, however I am not sure the content is improving.

Although we have been converging for at least 150 years, remember that the information age of the computer is only a decade old in comparison with the telephone, which is a 125-year-old global cultural institution. If you buy into this cyclical generational anecdote, the telephone as a device is not scheduled to go away for another 15 to 25 years. History is on our side here.

Evolutionary convergence has brought the computer industry to point where this industry is not only open to telephony but wants to provide it as well. Computer companies are actively tapping new markets with computer and telephony types of applications – applications that model the transition of machines of computation to machines of communication.

Ignoring this trend is dangerous for those technologists who are responsible for understanding who their calling stakeholders are and how they go about making contact. If you don't understand this trend, you could very well alienate and disenfranchise tremendously important populations of callers. For example, fully 30 percent of the country still uses rotary dialing. If your enterprise is so digital that you cannot accept analog calls, and if some, all, or even a few of your stakeholders cannot call, you have a problem.

Even in the United States, where the PC has a pervasive presence everywhere, only 30 percent to 40 percent of American homes have a computer, compared with the more than 90 percent of homes that have telephones and televisions.

Telephone and television are the vehicles through which the mass market reaches the outside world.[2] One of the most underestimated communications phenomena driving the predominance of the telephone during the last decade was the fantastic upsurge of the 1-800 (and 888) number.

800 Numbers

Since AT&T introduced 800 service in 1967, call centers and 800-number toll-free services have long been intertwined. By some definitions, if your company has any toll-free, 1-800 numbers, you probably have a call center of some type.

- 80 percent of all businesses will have an 800 number by 1997. (source: SCAP)
- 800-number usage grew 250 percent from 1992 to 1994. (source: National Telemarketing, Inc.)
- in 1968, some 7 million 800-number calls were placed; in 1992, 10.2 billion.

The U.S. domestic telemarketing business, much of which is based on

800 numbers, grew from $400 billion in 1990 and will reach, by some estimates, $625 billion in the year 2000.

By May 1993, only 26 years after its introduction, the 800 industry had used roughly 40 percent of the available numbers. By May 1995, approximately 80 percent of the available 800 numbers had been used. The new 800-number service, the 888 prefix, will provide about 7.6 million new toll-free numbers – the same amount as in the 800 series. After the usage of 800 comes 888; after those are exhausted, 877, then 866, then 855, and so on.

Did any single factor cause this explosion in consumption? Several probable factors include the implementation of 800-number portability across carriers, pager growth (to 27.3 million in 1995), and the introduction of personal 800 numbers for residences.

Ultimately, the reason for the toll-free number explosion can be traced to one factor: the phone is so ubiquitous and reliable that businesses are expected to have a toll-free number or risk the cultural scathing of being hopelessly branded as technically anal-log. This reliability sets the standard – a rather significant crossover expectation.

The Reliability of the Phone

Few sounds ever produced in the history of man have been more consistent than the sound of dial tone. Let's face it, telephones are reliable. You have never had to re-boot your phone. The only reason you still need the phone is that you cannot beat its performance, and performance is a bandwidth issue. The same with phone systems.

Omaha, Nebraska has been the mecca of call centers since the late 1960s. Omaha had an excellent nuclear-proof telephone infrastructure because of the headquarters of the U.S. Air Force Strategic Air Command. The local phone companies recognized their technological advantage and actively solicited companies that needed reliable (the central office switches of Omaha were designed to withstand a nuclear

51

attack) and over capacitied infrastructure on which to build large reservation centers.

Reliability is paramount. Although network technology has quickly come a long way, the only guaranteed way to hold a reliable, fully duplexed conference call with persons in Paris, London, Hong Kong, and Silicon Valley is by phone.

Despite marketing hype from the LAN and client/server industry about delivering PBX services and functionalities, people still think of the phone company, not Novell, when they want phone services. I do not expect to see the complete consumption of PBX features by servers for a long time.

The History of Convergence

Not only is the phone historically embryonic in its technical impact; it is tied closely to the convergence of computer-based telephony. Following is a map that outlines the migration of the great technical harmonic convergence, otherwise known to many as CTI. This map can be applied to almost any rapidly advancing technological industry, including health care, law, and financial services.

Mainframe
    Minicomputer
        Micro PC
            Sound Cards
                CD ROM
                    Multimedia
                        Client/Server
                            Computer-based Telephony
                      Auto Number ID
                  Mobile Communications
                Voice Mail
            Paging
        TouchTone
      Self-dialing
    Operators

The Parallel (Processing) of ENIAC

Any information system manager or executive understands that being skilled in both telephony and computing is highly leveragable. To some extent, the unquestioned reliability of the telephone has bred a form of arrogance in the telephony community. Too often, telecom people do not give enough credit to descendant history of the computer and its significant influence on our current period of convergence.

The relevance of the Electronic Numerical Integrator and Computer (ENIAC) on the telecommunications industry hit home resoundingly for me at a telecommunications conference on February 14, 1996. I was attending Jerry Goldstone's (publisher of *Business Communications Review*) PBX96 Conference. In spite of two stories on the front page of USA Today, not a single speaker, presenter, or telecommunications executive acknowledged that that particular day was the 50th birthday of the world's first computer. In 1946, the 30-by-50 foot ENIAC weighed in at 30 tons and was equipped with 18,000 vacuum tubes, 6,000 switches, and 3,000 blinking lights. Another unmentioned irony was that during the conference, the world's ranking chess master, Garry Kasparov, was battling IBM's Deep Blue supercomputer in a duel of the digits.

Deep Blue has a silicon and gold brain the size of two refrigerator-sized, 16-node parallel-processing computers. The computer program is so complex that even Deep Blue's handlers admit they rarely understand how it arrives at any given decision. In three minutes (the time allotted for each move in a formal chess match), Deep Blue can consider more than 20 billion moves (20 billion seconds would equal 620 years). Deep Blue won the first game but lost the match. One of Deep Blue's developers expressed amazement that this computing ability was still not enough to beat a mere human. The implication is that chess masters such as Garry Kasparov are performing some mysterious computation that cannot be figured out. At one point during the fourth match, Deep Blue crashed, but the IBM team had re-established contact with the machine in Youngstown Heights, New York within 15 minutes.

During the several-day event, many people tried to access Garry Kasparov and the Deep Blue World Wide Web site that was covering the event. Many people were rejected and turned away. The WWW site was swamped over the weekend between games one and two, and "browsers" encountered frustrating busy signals and connection failures. Even though IBM originally built the site to support more than 200,000 hits per day, they had not expected that by Sunday of the 10-day match, the site would have registered more than 5 million hits. IBM apologized profusely for the inaccessibility and, by the third game, had added six more SP2 supercomputers, the same type as Deep Blue, to handle Internet demand. The fact that not a single one of the 30,000 telephone complaints per hour that IBM received about the Internet connection was blocked has never been mentioned.

Deep Blue was designed ostensibly to conduct research to show how parallel processing can be harnessed to solve the types of complex problems and applications found, for example, in airline call centers, such as forecasting fare changes (up to 300 per hour), calculating skills-based routing matrices, and load scheduling.

Eventually this same computing power will be delivered to the desktop of the consumer, both at work and at home. In the past, cybercontact was constrained by the availability of processing power. Now bandwidth is emerging as kingmaker, and the day is not far off when the computer and the telephone will become a single, multipurpose appliance. The PC will evolve into an information appliance much more like the telephone rather than vice versa. A defining characteristic will be that this device is never turned off, as much as the telephone is always turned on.

How Is It Going to Get There?

Evolution of the capability to deliver bandwidth to the masses is the guidepost by which to set the pace of the development of your customer technology solutions. After almost 30 years of the Jetsons on television, and 2001 and Star Trek in the movies, we are driven culturally to obtain and integrate into our lives full-motion, two-way interactive dialogues between everybody. Once this "video dial tone" standard is established universally, the technology of customer service's growth will be incremental, not revolutionary, and most changes that occur will reflect quality, not quantity.

We are coming to understand that technology changes rapidly over many years. To grasp how limited we are at transmitting real-time data to the masses, we can look at the modes of transmission available currently and their rates of data transmission. For example, T1 is a high-speed data link that can broadcast about 1.5 million bits per second, 53 times faster than the 28.8 Kbps modem, but can cost up to $1,800 a month plus an installation fee as high as $3,000. The cost, not the technology, is what keeps T1 from being deployed to the home.

Cyberselling needs speed and bandwidth. But the speed available today for the consumer is prohibitively expensive, and typical phone lines are insanely and comically slow compared to what can be provided using available technology. As a culture, we are simply ignorant and do not know it because we have never had anything else available. The following chart presents the relative differences among the information transmission modes that are becoming and will be available over the next five years.

Transmission times for images through different systems[3]				
	Standard Analog Phone Line	ISDN Phone Line	ADSL* or T1	Cable Modem†
Simple still image (2 megabytes)	1.2 minutes	35.7 seconds	1.3 seconds	.5 seconds
Complex still image (16 megabytes)	18.5 minutes	4.8 minutes	10.7 minutes	4 seconds
Short-animation video (72 megabytes)	1.4 hours	21.5 minutes	48 seconds	18 seconds
Long-animation video (4.3 gigabytes)	3.5 days	21.4 hours	48 minutes	18 minutes

*ADSL (Asymmetrical Digital Subscriber Line) and T1 are different systems that have approximately the same transmission capabilities. The T1 technology can be used with fiber-optic or regular phone lines, while ADSL is an experimental technology designed to use standard phone lines but not expected to be available until about 1998.

†Cable modems are expected to be available by cable companies in 1997 and to be available by retail in 1998.

We will know that we have arrived when the full-motion videophone becomes a standard appliance like the telephone. In fact, the bandwidth issue is the most direct influence over the 30-plus years of Picturephone history. The Picturephone has been around for a long time and serves as a prominent example of the rapid pace of long-term technological change.

The Picture-esque History of the Picturephone

Video appears to be the next logical step in the evolution of call centers. Video is definitely coming, if only to preserve the face of the agent as the interface (no pun intended). Though the telephone has made a profound impact on the way humans have interacted for generations, we now understand that only 7 percent to 10 percent of all information communicated is verbal; a whopping 90 percent of communication is facial and expressive. Despite the overwhelming 30-year history proving the viability of the Picturephone, its acceptance has been slow in coming.

1964 AT&T shows the Picturephone at the New York World's Fair.
1970 AT&T offers Picturephone for $160 per month.
1973 AT&T drops Picturephone.
1982 Compression Labs sells a $250,000 videoconference system using $1,000/hour lines.
1986 PictureTel unveils a $80,000 videoconferencing system using $100/hour lines.
1987 Mitsubishi sells $1,500 still-picture home phone.
1989 Mitsubishi drops the still-picture phone.
1991 PictureTel unveils a $20,000 videoconferencing system that uses $30/hour lines.
1991 IBM and PictureTel demonstrate a videophone in a PC.
1992 AT&T announces another attempt with a $1,500 videophone for the home market.
1994 Scientists from Cornell University develop popular CU-See-Me Internet software.
1995 A videophone for less than $200 is delivered by Connectix.
1996 Several Korean computer makers make videocamera standard at less than $200.

Video prices are falling rapidly. I anticipate that 1997 will be the year when we start to see videotelephony at consumer price points. Intel's video-on-a-chip product now sells for $1,500 for a new system, already down from $2,000 as little as four months ago. Intel supplies 80 percent of the microprocessors used in the world's PCs, a fact not to be ignored by anyone watching the pace of the impending consumer two-way interactive video revolution.

For those with Windows PCs equipped for multimedia – including microphone, sound, and videoboards – the cost of cameras and software will have fallen below $200 and will be standard equipment by the end of 1997. Compaq and IBM now bundle these new video systems in their PCs, removing much of the complexity from the installation process. Compaq is the first PC maker to offer video, but these systems require Intel's Pentium chip with speeds of at least 133 megahertz. The video "screen" itself measures only four-by-five inches, and the picture is of relatively low quality, although quality will improve with the advent of high speed modems. Also, the software for the camera is still complex and far from "plug and play." And, of course, phone connections (ISDN or POTS) are always unreliable.

However, these limitations will be overcome in a short time and, within five years, every PC will contain a camera as standard equipment. Many forecasters predict that, as prices drop and quality improves, videocommunications will sneak up on the consumer mass market just as fax did in the 1980s.

Consumers, particularly executives in technology companies, have started to use these video-augmented systems at home. Already we have a $200 million-plus desktop videoconferencing market, enough of a critical mass to push the sale of video interaction out of the doldrums of the past 20 years. In fact, the growth of video can be tracked along the classic hockey stick growth curve.

Sales of PC-based Picturephones, in millions of units:

1993 - .006
1994 - .03
1995 - .1
1996 - .75
1997 - 2.5[4]

Videoconferencing, mostly business based, has tripled annually for each of the last three years (1993 through 1995). In 1995, fewer than 100,000 desktop videoconferencing systems were sold worldwide, less than one percent of all personal computers sold.

In addition to the chips that have the horsepower to process video signal, the pipeline that carries the signal is important. Video requires a faster and larger pipeline than that which regular phone lines can offer. Currently most users of interactive video employ (video slow) ISDN lines.

Coming soon from Intel will be video that can run on POTS. This new generation of video systems will use regular phone lines operating on 28.8 Kbps modems, the fastest practical modems available.

A major drawback to video technology is the quality of the picture. Desktop video is a long way from matching television quality; it runs at 10 to 15 frames per second, while television runs at 30 frames per second, creating images that are so herky-jerky the novelty wears off in less than five minutes. The quality is horrible and, for all practical purposes, you cannot make out facial expressions, defeating the very attribute and benefit video should deliver.

The quality issue results from the fact that all desktop video images that move over regular phone lines, both ISDN and POTS, must be heavily compressed and then decompressed. Each time a compression or decompression occurs, the quality of the image is degraded.

Television uses a noncompressed signal; because of television, we have a cultural bias toward television-quality pictures. Until we achieve the same television quality on our PCs as we have on our TVs, high quality two-way interactive video will remain unaffordable by the consuming masses and rented (not purchased) by the business masses compelled by their companies to use it.

Certainly, in time, PC video quality will come to match TV quality, but do not expect television quality at the desktop anytime soon (at least three years). However, call center technologists need to watch, peripherally, several other industries and, particularly, the desktop video collaboration technologies. Experience in two-way interactive video will be driven from there.

Some leading-edge pundits are saying already that the latest paradigm-busting technology has arrived in the form of video on demand. The closest, however, that most consumers can possibly come to the archetype of Star Trek-quality two-way video is with ISDN.

In the long run, ISDN will prove to be the cultural burden that the fax has become. ISDN represents the epitome of the narrow-band technologies of today. Not only is ISDN expensive, often costing $500 to install and $30 to $50 per month to use, but it is obnoxiously difficult to install and utilize. Also, the farther you are from the major metropolitan population centers, the less sophisticated the available technical support, and the less likely it is that the user will have a high degree of technical knowledge. Installing ISDN in the middle of the boondocks can be an exhausting experience.

But to offer and gain acceptance for video, you need users and, in particular, users who have PCs. The reality of it is that there are neither as many PC owners out there as Microsoft would like us to believe, nor will there ever be. Analysts predict that the explosive market for personal computers in U.S. homes of the last several years is poised to stall next year, before actually *beginning to subside* in 1998.

Market research firm Dataquest, Inc. expects that the home PC market is on the verge of being tapped out as many people who can afford to do so have already purchased a computer. Dataquest forecasts that the number of PCs shipped to U.S. homes will increase by 8 percent this year over 1995, while stalling to flat growth in 1997 and dropping by two percent in 1998. In 1995, Dataquest said that home PC shipments surged 22 percent following a 42 percent jump in 1994. The market is approaching saturation among households earning more than $100,000 a year, but interestingly, only about 1 in 10 individuals earning less than $30,000 owns a PC.[5]

It is not insignificant that the cost of a PC is well below $1,000. But the unanswered question is whether anybody who would spend $500 for a PC really wants one. The telephone works just fine for a huge portion of our population. Nevertheless, cable TV has a greater penetration in some areas than does the telephone, specifically, in some of our ghetto communities. Cable modems present an interesting challenge when trying to forecast the cable TV influence on the future of the device.

Cable TV vs. PC

While Web aficionados grind along, using slow modems and cramped phone lines – a combination that often requires minutes to download a single Web page – cable modems today can download information at 10 megabytes per second, or more than 350 times faster than the 28.8 Kbps modems available for PCs. However, the starting price for a cable modem at $500 each is just too much for the finicky home consumer to pay for a peripheral.

While cable modems and cable lines are speedy, the networks they are connected to are not. With the Internet's heavy traffic, some cable modem users are actually getting speeds of only 1.5 megabytes per second, still 14 times faster than a 28.8 Kbps modem but slower than the 10 megabytes promised.[6] That is like a cocktail straw feeding a firehose. And color is still too expensive, unless you use your TV.

The goal of the diverse interests of companies such as Motorola, Time Warner, Tele-Communications, Sun Microsystems, Intel, and Netscape is to make consumers view the WWW as a different kind of TV, an interactive TV with a million channels. But keep in mind that the cable companies are not out to sell you TV content; they want your phone service. They want a slice of the $300 billion telecommunications industry.

As evidence that we are groping for a universal multifunctional device, Oracle is planning the first public demonstration of a low-cost appliance-like computer intended for Internet access called a network computer (NC). The NC would sell for less than $500 and will be virtually a stripped-down PC with only a microprocessor, memory, and modem but no storage devices. You will run software from and store data from the Internet, using one or more service providers as a central network computer, or server.

To be truly successful and economically efficient, the call center requires an appropriate level of technology capable of matching not only the sociological but the technical diversity of the customers who call. The interactive nature of the Internet and the high-speed transaction processes made possible by cable modems all will influence how customers and stakeholders will expect to engage you in their contacts.

Conclusion

From computers that recognize speech and handwriting to the information superhighway and the worlds of virtual reality, the digital revolution is transforming the way we live, work, and relate to each other.[7] Let's put this TV, PC, and NC thing into perspective.

As of 1996, these were the facts of telecommunications devices:

- 10,000 interactive TVs in the United States
- 50,000 screen phones
- 28,000 new cellular subscribers per day
- 15 million with WWW access
- 20 million PCs with modems
- 250,000 PBX phone systems in the United States
- 300 million people with telephones.

More than one million PBXs operate worldwide; 225,000 of these are in North America.[8] Of all of the PBXs sold in the United States in 1995, one quarter had ACD functions.

The global PBX market is a $20 billion-a-year business. The United States alone accounts for $6 billion. The investment in core PBX products is more than $25 billion in North America. A total of $40 billion has been invested in our domestic telecommunications infrastructure; this includes applications such as voice processing, call accounting, and call center and systems management.

An expansive foundation is being laid for a new and exciting communications infrastructure for the next century. Through this infrastructure, computers can access and present information in exciting new and flexible ways. Computers and telecommunications can bring the richest information resources from the largest libraries right to the middle of the smallest town.[9]

No doubt exists that PBX technology, architectures, and applications are in a period of change more profound than the transition from analog to digital systems a decade or more ago. And yet I will predict that, if history is any indication, the telephone as a device is not scheduled to go away for another 20 years. Fully 30 percent of the nation's phones are still rotary.

Available downtime per year for the public network is six seconds. Providing a dialtone all of the time requires incredible reliability and redundancy. Are we in North America ever really more than just a phone call away from help? Most people know that their phone is still far more reliable than their PC. A poison control center has no need for a home page on the WWW for taking emergency calls but may want to make all of the poison control information available that way for research and information.

After a short burst of excitement, people will respond more slowly to the idea that the PC will supplant the telephone as the primary communications device on the desktop or anywhere. Consumers will not be able to watch TV-quality video over normal phone lines until the phone companies offer either broad band phone lines or ultrafast digital cable lines.

Overall, our species, while full of animated analysts and technology enthusiasts, is definitely pragmatic and generally slower than we think to change our course of technical evolution. The faster things change, the more they consistently stay the same.

As far as the customer and stakeholder callers are concerned, voice and data will remain separate mediums for a while longer – at least 10 more years. Even on the Starship Enterprise, Captain Kirk and crew carried both voice communicator badges and tri-corders, one for voice and the other for data.

But watch the PC market as it begins to ship PCs with powerful Digital Signal Processors (DSPs) and Codecs, quickly making available real-time voice and video. Groupware is one industry discipline that will continue to grow as a driver of innovative and sophisticated call center applications. Lotus Notes will prove to be a demonstrable precursor to the integration of pure, real-time multimedia communication.

On the business side of the stakeholder equation, the call center will become virtual and eliminate all boundaries. The call center in the new world order will span the entire enterprise, and everyone will be an agent. In this call center, the common element among the population of workers and agents will be a single, common integrated desktop device. The future of this appliance will involve accepting the fact that business communications operate under a different set of rules than do personal communications. These rules of engagement, or operational entanglement, will govern the conduct of the stakeholder contact. For example, most business callers value efficiency over pleasantries. These rules are so complex that the only "computer" smart enough to deal with them is with the sophisticated automation provided by agents, the human factor in the call center technology equation.

---

[1]Geng, Carl. (1996, Feb. 12). Keynote speech. Seimens Rolm, PBX96 Washington, DC.

[2]*Personal Technology,* WSJ, Walter Mossberg, June 13, 1996, B1.

[3]Source: Forrester Research Inc.

[4]Telespan Publishing Company. (1996, Feb. 25). *Wall Street Journal,* B6

[5](1996, March 19). *Wall Street Journal,* B3.

[6]Rogdon, J. (1996, March 28). "Blurring the line. New Technology Aims to Make the Web Like Television." *Wall Street Journal,* R20.

[7]Farrington, G. (1996, March). "ENIAC: The Birth of the Information Age." *Popular Science,* 74.

[8]BCR (BCR 4/94)

[9]Farrington, G. (1996, March). "ENIAC: The Birth of the Information Age." *Popular Science,* 76.

THE HUMAN AGENT
OR THE AGENT HUMAN

Discipline and concentration are a matter of being interested.
– Tom Kite

Although possibly able to warm some of the hearts in an increasingly alienated world, technology will never substitute for human contact. Personalized answers and intimate, relationship-building interactions occur only when the caller is connected to the agent. For the most part, in every enterprise it is the call center that now does the handshaking with customer and stakeholder callers.

The metaphor of the handshake describes perfectly the role of the call center in today's enterprise. As humans, we greet each other by touch or by signs that validate our attempt to communicate and understand. The handshake represents the survival of the ancient custom of creating a truce by taking hold of the weapon hand to insure against treachery, thereby preventing meeting adversaries from stabbing one another. This custom has led to the modern form of greeting, which is appropriate for the call center because the message "Let's communicate meaningfully" must permeate any dialogue between you and your caller.

The "handshake with the call center" is the identification stage. How do we automate that? Who else can give you that friendly handshake other than a human agent? No intelligent machine or technology can sum up a customer's attitude better than the agent. People are still servicing

65

customers. You can shift the responsibilities for those matters that really require people because you need their judgment.

The idea that the call center can provide the handshake and the ears for an entire business is not so far-fetched any longer. All contact between the world and the business is channeled through trained spokespersons, not always called agents and not always from a formal call center. Whatever the descriptor, these trained spokespersons may often be undervalued, but are extremely critical as primary resources in the enterprise.

Corporate America is catching on. By the end of 1995, approximately 4.5 million people worked for call centers. By 2000, that figure is estimated to increase to 10 million workers, an astounding three percent of the population![1]

Meet the professional call center agent, who goes from one call center job to the next. The demand is increasing for call center professionals. Some Canadian community colleges even have formally accredited educational and training programs for call center personnel.

More calls are placed now than ever before, and the trend will continue for the next 15 years. Automation is in a position to accommodate the brunt of the growth, but I do not envision the size or requirement for the agent population diminishing. We shall be able to support the increased call volume without adding as many agents as we would have without the automation. For example, shortening the average time a caller is engaged by giving the agents better tools would help us get the headcount down for the same call volume or absorb a higher volume with the same headcount. I think the latter is more likely.

How much of that human element will go away, and how much of it will be automated? The line will be drawn at the point where companies recognize that the mechanisms of automation are denying the enterprise the opportunity to talk to its customers and stakeholders, to make new sales, and to solve problems efficiently. Companies are recognizing that some situations lend themselves to automation, such as just providing a service when the chances of making a sale are practically zero anyway. But many situations do not, and for organizations with automated customer solutions, these pose a real problem.

If automation even begins to interfere with sales or productivity, organizations will revert reflexively to having humans answer the phone. Human things still have to be done. You cannot just plug automation in and have an instant digital solution in a can. Inevitably, the human being will remain the most "plug and play" of all computing systems for many years to come.

Technology does not replace people in the process here. People are essential to the process, but their knowledge – their ability to use information tools and to communicate that knowledge in a commercial form – is what matters, not headcount.[2] Generally, you can call and talk to a CEO or VP in the most technically advanced companies, particularly in healthcare and financial service industries, without too much difficulty. You can always reach a VP. Because the telephone will not go away, the agent person becomes the single most important source of contact in your company; like military effectiveness, you never leave the front line troops lacking anything.

The only thing that keeps people waiting on hold for any length of time is a person. The agent will never go away. Agents will be less involved and will be used selectively, but they are not going to go away. You still need to have a living person help you in many situations: for instance, language or intelligence difficulties; or the caller may be confused or old.

One of the defining trends is that the agent is going to be a decision maker ("Yes, I will fix that for you. I will correct that error."). The contact becomes a problem-solving and action-taking engagement as opposed to, "That's what the database says; take it or leave it."

With automation and technology like voice mail, people seem almost startled when they encounter a human voice on the other end of the line, but the fact is that a machine cannot empathize with the caller in a service environment.

The diminishing role of operators is a good example of the increasingly pervasive use of technology. Operators today sit in front of powerful workstations. Each operator can now handle 650 to 700 calls per day. Society's first call center agents plugged calls into manual "cord boards." Since then, rotary phones have given way to push-button models to cordless and ubiquitous cellular phones.

AT&T announced in September 1996 that they would close the last of what were once 15 AT&T operator systems in New England. After more than a century, the operator is quietly fading away, along with receptionists and bank tellers. Estimates suggest that in a few short years, only 100 operators nationwide will remain. In 1984, AT&T had 40,000 operators; today, fewer than 8,000. Of all the calls AT&T handles, 90 percent are made without operators.

According to George David, CEO of United Technologies Corporation, 18 million U.S. workers hold jobs that are easily prone to automation.[3] In Pittsburgh, Nortel-equipped companies provide 98 percent-accurate speaker recognition for directory services. Telephone operators belong to a job sector that is rapidly disappearing.

Because customers are more sophisticated than ever, they require a sophisticated response from a sophisticated agent. If wage is any indicator of technical savvy, a study by Princeton economist Alan Kruger found that people who use computers at work earn on average 15 percent more than those who do not. A huge population consisting of an experienced, decentralized, enabled work force is emerging. The higher-paying jobs are going to the computer savvy. Without better education and skills, many Americans face a bleak future in the knowledge-based, information-driven economy that is evolving.

"Human skills are subject to obsolescence at a rate perhaps unprecedented in American history," said Alan Greenspan of the Federal Reserve Board. High technology – not international trade imbalance – is the real force behind the widening gulf between the pay of a skilled knowledge worker and that of an unskilled worker. Millions of jobs have been altered beyond recognition since computers became commonplace at the desktop. Agents today must be able to use database technologies to access customer profiles, navigate among systems, and respond to triggers and business rules.

Progress is inevitable and will displace millions. But those who no longer dig ditches by hand or take orders by telephone either must find work in companies that need more complaint handlers or more managers to oversee product and service quality and customerization, or must use these empowering technologies to build their own livelihoods.

In his book *Being Digital*, Nicholas Negroponte contends that very significant values are being created by knowledgeable, skilled people moving "bits" almost costlessly through the appropriate systems. The old high-cost, labor-intensive model (of manufacturing goods based on "atoms" and then transporting and trading all those physical atoms) is being obviated, at least in those few high-end businesses that are beginning to re-consider the strategic importance of their technology for customer contact.

An example of what is occurring here can be seen in the rapidly growing call center application of telephone triage. At least one half of emergency room visits are not necessary, wasting up to $7 billion annually. An innovative solution is the use of 800-number medical call centers that patients can call before they head to the emergency room. One company has 175 registered nurses who field an average of 35 calls per day. For example, a caller with abdominal pain visits with a nurse who pulls up a checklist of questions from her PC under the heading of abdominal problems.

These services result in more than half of all callers recieving less expensive and less intrusive treatments. Prudential Insurance Company found that 8 of 10 callers were diverted from the emergency room.

The power of call centers is empowering and leading the way toward a medical era in which "information doctors" will specialize in caring for people over the phone. Pundits ask, "How can you deliver complex, detailed medical advice over the phone?" I am not certain why we cannot considering that we already do this for our PCs, and they are certainly as sophisticated.

The smart companies are recognizing that there are some things that lend themselves to automation. But it is a real problem when companies stand between themselves and their customers with an automated solution that denies them the mechanisms to talk to those people and make a new sale or provide intimate personalized service.

Crossover Expectations

Crossover expectation does not exist in most industries. If I go to a grocery store and have a wonderful experience and then go to a car dealership and have a bad experience, I do not (often, anyway) ask myself, "Gee, why can't I get the same great service at the dealership as I got at my grocery store?" I know of few exceptions to this, but one applies to any company that has a call center.

Ignoring the effect of crossover expectations is a trap into which many companies fall. It is instinctive to compare the handshake of your company with that of others in your same industry. Customer expectations, however, are driven by the influence of crossover expectation. You would do well to think like a consumer when designing your company's call center routing matrices.

Ten years ago, for a company to front-end all of their customer communication with some type of technology was unthinkable. However, how many companies now actually front-end their technology with a live person?

For now, technology must be placed up front because of the sociological fact that once a human being comes on the line, a customer caller will resist being transferred and most will, in fact, be insulted if they are. Once a live person has answered, you can rarely transfer the caller to a machine.

Ideally, we would route all calls through a "human triage," where an agent decides the direction of the call, including the option of sending the caller to a machine such as an IVR. In reality, this works infrequently because of crossover expectations.

Perhaps no industry other than the computer hardware and software industry tries to thoroughly understand and keep up with the psychology of its callers.

At least once in every computer owner's life he or she must bite the bullet and call technical support. Shakespeare once said something like, "Hell hath no fury like a 'caller' scorned." Studies prepared by Robert Johnson of Dataquest, show that only one in seven customer-support calls at midday even get through to a customer-support technician. Approximately 85 percent of these calls reach a busy signal.

Microsoft receives about 750,000 calls for help from customers every month. That represents nine million frustrated callers a year. Symantec's 505-employee Customer Service Center in Eugene, Oregon fields 15,000 calls per day. IBM answers 200,000 calls daily. Third-party support lines field another estimated 100,000 calls per month. Added to this figure must be the approximately 500,000 calls each month to every other call center for technology support.[4]

Hundreds of thousands of customers hang up before they get help because they do not know how long they will be on hold. Gradually callers will no longer hear the well-worn response, "Thank for calling, all of our agents are busy assisting other customers. . . please hold and your call will be answered in the order received"; they will hear the active, engaging dialogue of queue jockeys (QJs). Radio Symantec's three QJs play pop music and offer live wait time updates for callers in Symantec's three dozen telephone queues.[5]

The idea behind QJs is to set customer expectations and bolster customer loyalty. Because so many of us listen to the radio while we drive, radio is fast becoming the emulated format for engaging customers and getting them to wait comfortably during extended hold times. For example, Radio Delrina is the name of a Toronto company's live telephone service for customers on hold.

Microsoft pioneered the concept of on-line disc jockeys for waits that can last 45 minutes or more for Word for Windows help. I am not certain any connection exists between the following anecdote and the reason that listening to a QJ makes the time on hold go much faster, other than the fact that both cater to the dynamics of human nature and our propensity for substituting activity for achievement.

A tall building in Chicago was renovated with supposedly much faster elevators. Within several days, the tenants complained that the elevators were in fact terribly slow. Within several months, the presence of a serious problem was evident. The building's management brought in top experts from the elevator company to figure out how to speed the elevators up (and down). They looked at many different options, several of which were very expensive, including adding additional elevators or new motors. After many months of consideration and cost analyses, a young engineer suggested that they install mirrors in the lobby of each floor. The theory was that once people had something to do – stand there and look at and groom themselves – they would not notice the extended length of time they were waiting for the arriving elevator. Complaints

72

dropped by more than 90 percent within several months.[6] The desire for human contact and the results it can provide will explain the enduring need for call center agents.

More often agent responses require innovative, spontaneous solutions. I talked recently with a technical-support person from Company A who suggested that we call and conference in a technical-support agent from Company B who might have something to do with the problem we were resolving. Between the two of them, they fixed my problem quickly. My problem was solved by agents from two different companies, who sometimes compete with each other but collaborated in that instance to help me.

Are your agent employees creative? Are they working in an environment where they can slow down to do things that require more judgment and take more care?

My Very Own Agent

A notion is incubating with call center technology about a transformation from agent anonymity to agent intimacy. I would get the same agent every time I call and, in time, the agent comes to know the caller/stakeholder personally.

Is agent familiarity, where I contact consistently the same agent, a realistic expectation for building a relationship? The concept of the same agent every time is largely another vendor creation that sounds consequential in theory but is unlikely to yield any substantial value for several reasons.

First, just getting a live agent most of the time is tough enough, much less getting the same agent. The trade-off for getting the same agent every time is the potential delay in waiting for that individual. Even sophisticated technology for QJs and calculating the average wait time do little good in stopping a certain percentage of callers from abandoning their calls.

As a caller, I would be happy to reach the same person, but I want the next alternative available instantly. Most populations of callers will not wait around. Unless you are working between defined work periods of time, the hit rate will be low. When the customers call in for the second time, the chances of the most familiar agent being available to them at that time are relatively low, except in small office/home office (SOHO) environments.

Furthermore, if you have the right kind of CTI in place, rarely will any caller need to talk to the same agent. The caller will learn that a different agent is informed about the problem, and your file is very clear to anybody who answers the phone. While the customer may feel at first a little uncomfortable about talking to other people who say, "I know everything, I can handle this for you," as soon as they prove that they do and they can, being digital becomes a not-so-bad experience.

Keep Them Comfortable

Automate the repetitious, labor-intensive tasks where humans add no value. The uncontested prevailing driver for automation is the benefit of 24-hour-per-day, 365-day-a-year service. Unlike machines (for the most part), humans need breaks because they break down. You can always upgrade a computer, but you can rarely do more than maintain a human. The back affords a good example.

Each year, eight million new cases of back injury are reported. Almost 100 million workdays are lost annually because of back pain, and the average time to return to work after a back injury is 14 days.[7] Backaches are second only to colds and flu as the cause of lost work time in the United States. Repetitive stress injuries or cumulative stress disorders are 10 times more prevalent now than they were 10 years ago. Lost wages and medical costs from white collar injuries total $27 billion per year. The United States Occupational Safety and Health Administration says that motion and back injuries account for 30 percent of all worker compensation claims and projects an increase to 50 percent by the year 2000.

What does this have to do with call center workers? Agents sit for long stretches of time, work at their keyboards for hours, stare at a computer screen in a noisy workplace, breathe bad office air, and generally have stressful jobs. Backaches, repetitive stress injuries, eye strain, hearing damage, respiratory problems, and nervous stress are the results.

Investment in ergonomically supportive workstations for any population of workers, not only those in call center environments, yields long-term benefits. The most effective solutions revolve around taking short, periodic breaks in quiet, noncubical places.

Agent Empowerment

The demands on the customer-contact person are escalating. Correspondingly, those calls that reach the agents are becoming more challenging and complex. As a result, the agents must be given more responsibility and accountability.

This theory has different forms, such as ownership of the contact until closed, compensation incentives for up-selling and cross-selling, and skills-based payroll interface. Regardless, the more you know, the more you make. This requires a learning environment – the ability to earn while you learn.

Most agents want to do a good job, and have the customer's best interest at heart. With some exceptions, the average person wants to do a good job. You want the operational climate to be energized. You do not want to have bored employees engaged in uninteresting activities. Keeping agents and telephone-based employees moving at a pace that keeps them motivated should be a critical part of someone's responsibility.

The crucial application in the technologies of customer contact is bringing to the agents the information they need to make thoughtful processes out of a call. If they do not have this information, you have insulated the agent and you are not utilizing his or her intelligence. Automate the easy and leave the more difficult for the agent – not the other way around. In the past your agents have been automated robots;

they want to think. You will humanize them by giving them an opportunity to contribute. Give them decision-making flexibility. Provide enough information so the agent can make a decision regarding a complaint either at the champagne level or at the presidential suite level. An agent must be empowered to make these kinds of decisions.

The CFO of a large company walked into his company's bank and found the teller line too long for him to wait. He asked a teller to validate his parking ticket, and the teller replied that her management told her she could not validate his ticket without a transaction. The next day he returned and withdrew entirely all of his company's business. When asked why he was leaving, he explained that he didn't fault the teller – she was just doing her job; he faulted the bank's management for not empowering the teller with the ability to make a simple decision such as validating a parking ticket for a valued bank customer.

Given accurate information and authority, agents will make good decisions. However, agents who cannot respond to a customer's expectations will not be effective regardless of how much authority they have been granted. Because empowering the ground level agents and employees with this type of decision-making power may be hard for most companies, a recent alternative is having a "help desk" for the agents themselves, staffed with decisions makers.

Even if agents are given these powers, they are not really empowered unless support systems are in place to help them make good judgments. New applications empower agents with greater capabilities such as on-screen display of the latest queue statistics, timed return of calls to queue after no answer, keystroke macros for intelligent call-handling rules, single or multiline call answer, and automated outbound call handling. In addition, agents can access all formal call center features and functions from their keyboards, such as agent log-in, call supervisor, and activity code displays.

Cognitive Technology

Can we use technology to turn an unskilled person into a knowledge worker? Through vast databases of information, can we turn a telephone worker earning minimum wage into a well-paid knowledge worker? Can technology *make* a person a knowledge worker?

Yes, provided the calls to your company follow a well-defined pattern and a script can be developed to guide the agent through the contact process. What you leave for the human are the tasks the machine cannot do, which is to think, to make good decisions, to hear a sales cue and to jump on it.

But leaving the difficult tasks for the agent absolutely requires that he or she be capable of handling more difficulties. Besides all other types of callers, agents now end up with the caller who always chooses not to deal with the machine (and some subset will always do that if allowed).

With a work-flow and call-flow process and system technology implemented, agents throughout an organization can access the same central base of customer and product knowledge, whether they interface remotely through the Web or via a networked computer from their offices.

The lack of relationship between quality and talk time means that business phone calls operate under a different set of rules than do personal calls. Business callers value efficiency over pleasantries.

In these developing complex environments and connections, coordinated capabilities for voice and data transfer allow a caller's data to be transferred to another agent along with the voice call. An agent can now consult with another agent about a call while they both view application and customer data. On the surface, putting a caller on hold may appear an easy and simple decision for an agent. Closer examination proves otherwise, as various options must be considered.

For example, the agent may choose to put the caller on hold during the consultation (known as an immediate conference), to include the caller in the conversation with the second agent (a consultative conference), or to put the caller on hold initially and then add the caller into the consultative conversation. An agent may choose to put the caller on hold and consult with another agent before transferring the call and data (known as a consultative transfer). Or the agent may transfer the call and data without prior consultation (a blind transfer) or may transfer the application and data associated with the call without the call itself (a data-only transfer). And the options continue to multiply, making the decision that much more complex.

Learning Agents

Two forces work against agent generalization: lower cost call-processing technology and a movement toward handling ever more complex transactions by phone. As call centers handle more complicated transactions, the skills and knowledge required by agents increase dramatically.

In most call centers, an agent's role is complex and difficult. Extensive knowledge skills are required before an agent masters the job. Some centers gravitate toward following the high-level skill set and knowledge inventory: listening skills, speaking skills, call-control skills, typing skills, telephone and computer technical skills, product and service knowledge, courtesy and etiquette, policy and procedure knowledge, and skills in handling difficult callers.

The central management challenge for customer-intimate companies is to assemble, integrate, and retain talented people who can stay at the forefront of new paradigms and techniques that affect their stakeholders' businesses. An experienced agent is a highly skilled employee whose value is too high to waste on tasks that require no skills.

Employees most sought as agents have tremendous adeptness and deftness at effecting change within the caller. Employees with these skill sets are getting decent money when commissions, benefits, and salary are added together. We are seeing a migration to the agent with a core set of skills and competencies, a person who is multimedia enabled – a skilled knowledge worker.

Fully burdened labor easily costs the company $50,000 annually for one moderately skilled and moderately paid agent. Call center cost components are 60 percent personnel, 25 percent network, 10 percent overhead, and 5 percent equipment.[8] Fifty-four percent of customer service companies surveyed for the International Customer Service Association train newly hired customer service representatives for more than a week; about 20 percent train for one week; and 20 percent responded "other."

Are you training and enforcing agents to identify a buying signal? Can they spot alternate problems or issues? Can they recognize customer attitude? A well-trained, thinking agent will recognize a buying signal. An opportunity, for example, to submit a bid on homeowner's insurance. Can the agent convert the call into a potentially valuable cross-selling opportunity? If so, at the same time, by asking the appropriate questions, the agent can glean useful information from the customer. The key is getting information in front of the agent with which to identify the cross-sell opportunity.

Work and learning are becoming more one and the same – not learning for learning's sake but learning with a business purpose. Firms are going to have to become much more directly involved in education.

One of the biggest problems facing call center managers is simply keeping agents on the telephones. Many legitimate distractions can pull agents away from the phone: faxes, copying, interoffice correspondence, tracking down specific questions, accessing centralized files, and related tasks that are better left to clerical workers. Reports are the tool best suited to determine and monitor performance.

Reports

A natural conflict exists between productivity and quality in the call center. Productivity is easy to measure; quality is more elusive. And productivity no longer provides a competitive advantage. Plenty of call centers have shaved seconds off of calls. Most call centers are measured by the speed of the transaction and efficiency, but if the caller has to make three calls, they actually cost more than one long call that satisfies the caller's purpose in making the call in the first place.

In the past, because of legacy issues, you could not get detailed information on the productivity of each and every call. You would get summaries. For example, the prime statistic in call centers for years has been the average speed of answer or the percentage answered. As a customer I do not give a flip how long it takes as long as I get my problem resolved the first time. I will wait as long as necessary for me to be satisfied completely. But do we measure that? No, not very well.

We need choices as to how the system currently delivers support in real time vs. just moving averages ("sliding windows"). Executives dislike the loss of real-time data. Expectations about the availability of real-time data are driven from the data community, and the telecommunications vendors have only recently begun announcing robust real-time reporting capabilities.

The reporting capabilities of the system must enable the user to see reports in real-time or other variants. The most competent vendors have reporting down to less than three-second increments, as near to real time as you can get – almost empirical. Real-time display updates are actually real time. But when I log on from outside and do a network update, it is not real time. It has been engineered to two seconds; it is close, but there is a gap of two seconds. The gap depends on bandwidth.

Real-time and cradle-to-grave information must also now be reported. This means the beginning of a call to its termination – not just the agent's part of the transaction. A cradle-to-grave report covers every event that occurs throughout the entire call, even periods of waiting in queue, ring back, announcement, and transfer here-transfer there, and monitors each event as it goes across a distributing network of multiple nodes.

New generations of call reporting will see that every call will be tagged with an ID as it comes into the system, and that every call-processing step will be identified and tagged with that same ID. This event ID will include information about the time span of any specific action as well. Knowing the duration of each action of a call provides a powerful perspective. Call centers do count the number of calls collected in one contact, but now you need some objective way to measure the effectiveness of the whole application, to assess how it is being run. This includes the automated parts, the live parts, and whatever happens in between.

You are getting down to detailed programming of how to handle a call. You are talking about call-flow archiving or task-flow detailing. Two types of call reports can be used: reports on the callers and reports on the agents – task flows vs. specific actions. You are looking at the call "minutia" to see the profile of what is really going on. You are not burying the information in arcane, vague, statistical summaries. You are now differentiating calls more carefully, and you must figure out mechanisms for identifying call completion rates. You must go into the host computer and tap how many times this customer's file was pulled up this month.

Although we often presume that high quality always means the customer is right, this is unrealistic. The customer is not always right. Take, for example, a caller to a bank customer service organization who has just been notified of an overdraft situation. The caller will portray the telephone interaction as being poor no matter how the agent behaves, and calling metrics should be interpreted to reflect this type of situational variable. Sometimes the call center manager is shocked to realize that poor quality is the cause of rising call volumes and lengthening talk times.

In call centers related to health care, for example, people call and believe that they are talking to someone in their own company. The call centers that support these types of client contracts are based on certain guaranteed levels of service. Reports make it possible to ensure that nobody waited in a queue longer than a certain amount of time. If basic service includes 500 calls per month, then your company is billed for every call above that basic limit. For bill back, averages will not suffice. Without the details on the calls, you have no way to bill back.

We are talking about increasing the sophistication of reporting across multiple databases, the mixed reporting among data and host systems and ACD systems. This area offers considerable opportunity, and much energy is being spent here. The middleware vendors are really driving this stuff, bringing together diverse statistics from various places and creating a whole new set of reports that make sense. All the data are there. All of the call processing and data passed across any wide-area network can be broken into cradle-to-grave reporting elements.

Because of this, most vendors using client/server-based computing platforms will never have to take another complaint about the customer not liking their reports. All of the next generation of reporting products can be customized by a supervisor, or even by agents. The call center supervisor will see all the reports and can merely add a new call and put a calculation against a report and run it, just like a spread sheet.

One application requiring sophisticated reporting integration among different databases and systems is the payroll interface. Payroll interfaces are related to the function of getting away from the time clock and making the agents log in and log out the driver. If payroll time were measured with log-in and log-out timers, agents would be much more punctual, and many disciplinary problems would be avoided.

Payroll interfaces allow call centers to move away from grading agents on how fast they could handle each call, how closely they followed the script, and how much they shut off their phones to talk to their supervisor or run to the bathroom. Factory workers, even those on assembly lines, had a certain level of freedom that most telephone-based workers today do not have.

Payroll interfaces will become more important as compensation levels and incentive programs change. We will see more compensation based on performance, but performance in terms of selling, conflict resolution, and opportunities for customer satisfaction.

The general trend will focus less on how many calls are taken and how fast they are completed than on the result of the transaction. A call lasting twice as long but accomplishing three times more is much more effective.

In the future, performance measurement tools will be customized easily at the desktop. They will encompass not only average speed to answer and number of calls processed but more customer satisfaction-based metrics.

Therein lies the real future of call center performance measurement. A strategic technology executive will be more likely to ask you if the customers are happy than how many calls you have received. To accomplish this objective, we have the embryonic emergence of goals-based pacing for the agent population.

Conclusion

Intellectual capital is defined by Ernst and Young as material that has been formalized, captured, and leveraged to produce a higher valued asset. Some analysts who study knowledge management believe that, at best, only 20 percent of the intellectual capital inside a business is being tapped or utilized. The real profitability with the use of digital technology and call centers, together with new attitudes and values, lies in allowing enterprises to use more of their collective brain.

Customer-intimate companies need a broad set of skills and styles to get the job done. But little is more important than the skill of effecting a pleasant, positive handshake between company and customer. A new breed of sophisticated customer requires an advanced class of agent.

These agents must be adaptable, flexible, and multitalented; traits that allow them to deliver just about any reasonable or, sometimes, unreasonable response.

Our ability to tap into intellectual capital to yield wealth is growing. The drive toward high-quality, personal service mandates more effective access to information. Work is becoming an activity rather than a location. Networking will dramatically affect the physical location of the work force as the proximity of these knowledge workers to markets, plant, and other traditional locations becomes less necessary.

Most companies are trying to reinvent themselves for the new competitive, global marketplace. People and information are the most critical resources for this transformation. No resource is more capable of instantly recognizing a caller's needs and of acting on those needs than a live person. The ability to differentiate callers by their needs carries tremendous power. Sometimes technology is perfectly suited to allow callers to make some of the decisions themselves, however. In every organization, shareholders have different needs than do the deadbeats who don't pay their bills. To tell the difference requires empowering agents to know the difference, and it is the technology of the last five years that makes available the highly personalized customer information on which the future of one-to-one marketing rests.

---

[1]Sixel, L. (1995, May 13). "Texas Getting the Call". *Houston Chronicle*, 1D.
[2]Burstein, Daniel. (1995). *Road Warriors*. New York, NY, Dutton Penguin, 327.
(1996, April 22). Outlook. *Wall Street Journal*, A1.
[3]Churbuck, D. (1995, March 13). "Help! My PC Won't Work!" *Forbes*, 75.
[4]Kidd, J. (1996, Feb. 25). "QJs to Put Fresh Spin on Holding". *Wall Street Journal*, B3.
[5]Klenke, M. (1996, Feb. 22). Presentation notes. TCS, BCR PBX 96, Washington, DC.
(1996, March 13). Presentation notes. CT Expo, CenterCore for Ergonomic Research, San Francisco, CA.
[6]Reynolds, P. (1996). TCS Management Group.
[7]Zuboff, S. (1995). The Age of the Smart Machine.
[8]Stewart, T. (1994, Oct. 3). "Your Company's Most Valuable Asset: Intellectual Capital." *Fortune*, 32.

THE FUTURE OF ONE TO ONE

The next 10 years in computing are going to be driven by automating the consumer experience.
– Bruce Lupatkin

Americans already receive an average of 2,000 to 3,000 discrete commercial messages per day.[1] Most of this advertising exposes 800 and 888 telephone numbers (and WWW addresses). We can bet pretty safely that most of these numbers dial into a call center of some type.

Call centers are being depicted less as another business unit and more as a strategic asset. In the U.S. telemarketing industry alone, call centers and CTI technology support sales that exceed $400 billion a year.

Percentage of spending for advertisement by media in 1995[2]

Telephone Marketing	40%
Direct Mail	23%
Television	11%
Newspaper	10%
Magazine	5%
Radio	3%
Other Interactive Media	8%

This $400 billion worth of calls is generated from various sources. Telephone marketing is almost twice as prevalent as the next media used, direct mail.

I have often wondered, as I wrestle obnoxious chunks of junk mail out of my mailbox, why do they keep sending me all of this stuff? The reason we keep getting it is because we keep buying stuff from junk mail catalogs. Our generation is bombarded with junk mail. More than half of all people in America have ordered something from direct mail. Some surveys indicate that more than 80 percent say they find direct mail useful. That accounts for $385 million in direct mail each year.

But don't call it "junk mail"; call it "direct mail." Direct mail pays for itself and is not subsidized by Postal First Class postage rates. Direct mail is so important to the revenue of the U.S. Postal Service that the USPS is running radio commercials in major markets trying to convince the public to call these messages "direct mail" instead of "junk mail."

Junk mail and the volume of telephone-based traffic that it generates are just one example of a massive, generational trend from mass marketing to micromarketing. Although this trend may be far outside of their technical discipline, technologists must not ignore the impact of this sweeping shift in the global communications paradigm.

This marketing displacement will move dramatically from the one-to-many toward the one-to-one approach. The powerful new technologies of customer contact provide the basis for full-blown reordering of the huge retail and consumer spending sectors of the economy, both global and domestic. Mass media are being redefined by systems used for transmitting and receiving personalized information and entertainment. The technology of customer contact is evolving into a technology of dialogue.

Shouting! Marketing the Way It Has Always Been Done

The media of the future will allow you to communicate directly with your customers individually rather than shouting at them in groups. The most recent Superbowl drew an estimated viewing audience of more than 200 million people around the world. Television commercials during the Superbowl now command $1 million per 30 seconds during half-time.

Customers have lived through decades of progressively more adversarial mass marketing – the buy-or-die approach (if you don't buy this product now, you are missing out for life! Be like Mike. Obey your thirst.). Retreating from this adversarial challenge, selling communications and marketing communications as disciplines are now moving toward a collaborative transaction. Mass marketing has an acquisition motive; in contrast, pinpointed, individually targeted media intend collaboration. We are witnessing the death of the adversarial use of mass media, and we are redefining the arts of marketing and advertising.

Big bureaucratic advertising agencies are organized around messages to the masses, pitched to the lowest common denominator through the use of the trick, the tease, and the fashion statement. Flexibility is needed to deliver customized communications to niches. As markets and interests become more highly specialized, customers demand both style and substance. As niches narrow, the content must run deeper.

The thinking behind this trend relies on the popularity of "relationship marketing." This marketing concept supposes that you can remove the anonymity from the telephone call and create a lasting stakeholder relationship.

For at least the next 20 years, marketing communication will boil down to identifying and solving problems. In this context, you and your customer become collaborators. You are both trying to solve the customer's problem or meet the customer's need in a way that satisfies the customer and ensures a profit for you. This definition of customer service involves a significant element of verbal dialogue between the company and its customer. When call inquiries are linked to marketing campaigns and sales, the value of a marketing campaign in terms of revenue can be determined.

A study prepared by The Strategic Planning Institute and widely quoted by management guru Tom Peters showed that the "better" providers of customer service charged about 9 percent more for their goods, grew twice as fast, gained market share more quickly, and earned 12 percent return on sales. "Poor" providers earned only a 1 percent return on sales.

One-to-one marketing is driven by information technology and mandated by one-to-one media. What results is dialogue. Remember that dialogue is now possible because the computer can provide you with a foolproof memory of every customer's unique needs.[3]

Each media innovation has further reduced communications costs, making mass media (not mass marketing) advertising a progressively more effective way to publicize a product and generate transactions across a wide audience. Technology, primarily in the call center environment, is driving the paradigm shift from mass to micromarketing.

Three computer-enabled capabilities provide vital support for the new information age: 1) huge, detailed customer databases can be used to single out and remember individual customers and their preferences, 2) multimedia interactivity enables stakeholders to talk to you in a variety of ways, and 3) mass customerization allows you to provide an individually and specifically produced product or service to your stakeholders and customers. The technology of customer contact is, in fact, an operational entanglement that is based substantially on the technology of dialogue.

The Technology of Dialogue

Only since the mid-1990s have computer chips been small, cheap, and powerful enough to accomplish many of the tasks demanded of mass customerization. Call centers, at their cores, are semiconductor-driven growth industries that are suited ideally to serve the larger goal of creating customers for life. Companies that learn to use computer power to adapt each product or service to the needs of each single customer and that can produce in volume will have a nearly insurmountable advantage. (Some economists have predicted that technology will ultimately create only two players in every industry, a duopoly characterized by Microsoft and Intel.)

As information technology becomes cheaper, faster, and more accessible, even companies with relatively low-priced products and lower unit margins than today's stock commissions will begin to find it profitable to group their customers into portfolios and to assign responsibility for these portfolios to individual "customer" managers as opposed to "product" managers. The call center holds the prescription for building and individualizing caller relationships that are based on the management of caller needs, rather than wants. Technology drives the paradigm shift of information extraction from your customers to information exchange with individuals.

The interexchange carriers accommodated users by permitting them more digit patterns rather than actual numbers of trunks. Armed with this powerful feature, some users began to use the Dialed Number Identification Service (DNIS) to differentiate call processing not only by transaction types but by who did the calling. This gave the call center its first efficient way to engage in relationship marketing.

To get this kind of customer information in the past required outside databases, and third-party mailing lists. By the last decade of the 20th century, technical barriers no longer prevented you from knowing, in detail, the history of each of your stakeholders. Until recently, economic realities have only allowed large marketing departments to collect, analyze, and understand the data necessary to manage the customer side of the marketing space or to communicate with customers in a one-to-one fashion.[4]

The ability to remember a customer, from one event to the next, is the primary requirement for sustaining an ongoing relationship. As information and communications technology advances, individual customer communications and individualized dialogue management will become progressively more critical to any company's marketing success.

Chip size now enables us to "informationalize" products. To profit from the incredible shrinking microchip, begin to use information technology to incorporate memories of your customers into every conceivable aspect of your operations. The companies that make these products now have the ability to remember the tastes and preferences of almost every customer. Never require your customer or stakeholder to tell you the same thing twice.

I believe that most Americans would be shocked if they understand the tremendous detail these new biographic resources actually provide. Biographic leverage will be the tool of the next decade and is already used quite adroitly by a growing number of companies. Some people believe that most contemporary privacy issues revolve around not the big brother of government but around big brother's corporate cousin.

This metaphor may sound ridiculous today, but the time may not be too far off when nationally recognized retailers such as a Wal-Mart, Circuit City, or your grocery store record and track the dollar amounts and nature of your entire transactional history on-line and then cross-reference this with your income, your credit report, your medical and driving history, possibly a log of all of the e-mail you have ever received, and maybe even a list of all of the graphics you have ever pulled off of the Internet that have a flesh-tone content exceeding 30 percent!

The one-to-one marketing premise depends entirely on technological applications that support personal customer marketing. The databases hold the intimate knowledge of your customers and their needs. You must become adept at leveraging information from these databases – to map customers and their needs to the appropriate available resources.

In the spring of 1995, both the *Wall Street Journal* and the *Financial Times* reported that Netscape (makers of the popular Internet browsing software, Netscape Navigator) had received numerous customer complaints about a little-known, embedded feature called Cookies. Cookies allows Internet merchants to track what their customers are doing in their "stores" and how they are spending their time doing it, unbeknownst to the customer. A newer version of Cookies tracks customers' movements over days, weeks, months, and, as Martha Rogers predicts, even lifetimes. Ironically, the standards body for the Internet, the Internet Engineering Task Force, has reportedly asked Netscape to provide Cookies as a standard feature of the Internet.

Most firms have plenty of customer data, often stored in numerous databases that exist in separate and independent servers (for example, product development, groupware, e-mail, invoicing, warranty service, credit, delivery records, and accounting). Furthermore, customer data must be accurate and complete, immediately accessible, updated and adaptable in real time, and integrated with all the other data, applications, and systems.

The Pareto Customer

At the core of the emerging customer-intimate strategy is the Pareto principle. This principle is based on the idea that 80 percent of a company's business comes from 20 percent of its customers.

The Pareto rule comes in different forms: 20 percent of people do 80 percent of the work, 20 percent of the product generates 80 percent of the defects, 20 percent of the job takes 80 percent of the time, or 20 percent of the effort delivers 80 percent of the benefit. An often-cited corollary is that 20 percent of your customers require 80 percent of your time and effort.

Pareto was an Italian engineer and economist whose mathematical ability made important contributions to the discussion of the methodology of economics and to the role of that discipline in the social sciences as a whole. Pareto analysis is used to forecast and calculate the value of customers and stakeholders to determine and distribute the enterprise's resources, such as agents in a call center. The Pareto principle has two cousins, the "Law of Repeat Purchases" (the more you sell to any single customer, the easier it is to sell to him or her again) and the "Law of the

More Expensive Repeat Purchases" (the more you sell to any customer, the easier it is to sell to him again at a higher price).

Sophisticated permutations of the Pareto principle show that the best customers yield the highest margins and that this leads to lower advertising and marketing costs. Discounts, rebates, and other low-result, high-cost introductory processes can be reduced. The more a customer buys from you, the less likely he will be to buy from your competitor.

In the long-distance services business, the top 15 percent of customers consume 60 percent of services. In the United Kingdom, 6 percent of cola drinkers account for 60 percent of cola sales; in the car rental industry, 0.2 percent provide 25 percent of the revenues; at Pizza Hut, 10 percent of customers account for 30 percent to 40 percent of their profit.[5] James Vander Putten, a vice president for information management at American Express, says that the best customers outspend others by a ratio of 16 to 1 in retailing, 13 to 1 in the restaurant business, 12 to 1 in airlines, and 5 to 1 in the hotel business.[6]

Blockbuster Video has 40 million customer names, each identified with movie and video game preferences. They do not share their data with anyone. As a result, mass customerized movie and game promotions work very successfully. One initial mailing generated a response of 30 percent when the objective was 2 percent to 4 percent.

The technology of customer contact enables companies to differentiate individual customers, identifying those who are worth more than others. The cost of acquiring new customers is five times greater than the cost of retaining old ones; nevertheless, companies still spend an average of six times more money to acquire customers than they do to keep them. Most businesses lose about 25 percent of their customers annually through attrition. Any company that can eliminate just 5 percent off of that customer loss could add as much as 100 percent more profits to the bottom line.

Bottom line, a small number of your Pareto customers account for a significant percentage of revenue. Logically, a largely disproportionate amount of money should be spent on retaining those select customers from one transaction to the next because multiple transactions from the same customers are conditional events. Each successive transaction depends on each customer's continued satisfaction with the previous one. Every conversation with a particular customer must be built on the outcome of all previous conversations and interactions.

Proof lies in the fact. Being from a military family, I have been a USAA (San Antonio, TX) insurance policyholder for many years. Over those years, USAA has concentrated on retaining me as a Pareto customer, as I always receive prompt, accurate, and informed help with every transaction. I use USAA as a service standard against which to measure other call center experiences. My call center crossover expectations are pretty high as a result of my being treated as a Pareto customer by this company. Almost everyone would agree that USAA maintains a very high-caliber call center, as proven repeatedly by customer satisfaction surveys. But everyone believes that they also have a quality product.

Nissan believes that success requires producing not only a high-quality vehicle but also high-quality relationships with its customers – relationships that are focused attentively on complete satisfaction at every turn. Nissan discovered that providing a higher quality of service necessarily meant providing more personal, more individually relevant service that respected every customer's unique history of past contacts and transactions with the company.

The salient point is that most companies are probably overspending on customer acquisition and underspending on customer retention.[7] The antithesis is to reduce the total number of customers and nurture the business, which should increase profits.

The process of retaining customers relies entirely on technology to sustain beneficial communications with each and every contact. However, little efficiency can be found in striving for dialogue retention with every customer. No matter how feasible the technology, some customers are just not worth it.

Unload Your Losers

More than an instinctual action, kissing up to customers is a reflex. Firing customers is not a natural act, particularly so close to the '80s and early '90s heyday of the "Customer is King" movement. No longer is the customer necessarily the "king." The technology of customer contact now includes the ability to distinguish and identify not only those customers who are kings but those who are princes, a few minor nobles, and often a handful of common knaves.

In June 1996, a low-key, page B1 article in the *Wall Street Journal* described the discovery by the nation's ninth largest credit card issuer, Capital Financial Corporation, that only a small percentage of their customers accounted for more than one third of all toll-free calls. A significant number called at least once a day and at least one person made 700 calls in a single year (two a day, every day).

The irony in this story was the outrage expressed by some of these excessive toll-free users who received letters in "condescending tones" telling them to stop calling so frequently or Capital Financial would start charging for excessive calls. Cardholders were amazed when they were warned to call only when "truly necessary." Many were shocked to learn that Capital Financial tracked such data. One customer is quoted as saying, "It's scary to think that a company sizes up how good a customer you are not only by looking at your payment and employment history but also the number of times you call them."

The privacy issues are inherent in businesses' newfound abilities to track every detail of a long-term relationship with every customer and, for some, the privacy concerns are huge.[8] Normally, the on-line shopping mall software vendors try not to influence how their software is priced or how they promote their products. But the technology allows for detailed customer tracking and profiling data that enables retailers to target certain customers for specialized promotions.

Spending time and resources on a customer who offers absolutely no benefit to your firm is not worthwhile. Customer-driven companies will choose their customers deliberately, walking away from those who do not fit their visionary mold. They choose to narrow rather than broaden their operational focus. This awareness has led the larger integrated organizations to restructure themselves into separate units so that each can excel in its single discipline.[9]

Choose your Pareto customers carefully. Be careful not to fire the wrong customer. Sometimes it pays to just shut up and find out who your most obnoxious and irreverent customers are.

A back-page story that appeared in the Wall Street Journal on March 1, 1996, described a 71-year-old fellow named George Burke. Mr. Burke ran a successful advertising agency and product development company for 30 years, when he discovered a profitable niche selling black, steel, rolling bakery racks. The racks themselves turned out to be manufactured in Wilkes-Barre, Pennsylvania, by a $100 million company called InterMetro Industries Corporation. These shelves were ideal for use in retail display, medical storage, and other applications such as for bread, bagels, and hamburger buns. The shelves resist dust and promote air circulation. They were particularly ideal for stacking computers and networking equipment. Before long, Mr. Burke was buying $400,000 worth of racks a year from InterMetro.

Mr. Burke was constantly calling and contacting InterMetro with new product ideas and design recommendations. His contacts became so frequent and constant that, at one point, the company forbade the engineers who had brainstormed with him on a daily basis from taking any of Mr. Burke's calls on company time.

The company says that because their business was doing well, no one in engineering had time to deal with a demanding customer such as Mr. Burke. They felt also that George Burke's ideas, no matter how brilliant, were too customized and that the economies of scale "just aren't there."[10] Big mistake!

Identifying your best Pareto customers and then firing the rest is certainly not a process for the timid. Neither is increasing your remaining Pareto customer's expectations, one call at a time. Understanding how these customers want to be treated, how to "handshake" with them, is a key humanistic element in determining the architecture of the technology that supports these relationships.

How Customers Want to Be Treated

"Bad news" calls are the toughest to handle because the agent has no place to run. Training for this situation requires one of three options: 1) Apologize: "I am sorry you are having this bad experience." 2) Empathize: "I would feel the same way." 3) Offer a solution: "Let me suggest. . . ." All these responses are deliberate attempts to disarm hostile or negative callers, but any complaint is an opportunity to engage the customer in intimate dialogue.

Customers do not want to be treated equally; they want to be treated individually. This may sound like an overworked cliché, but you must view your customer as a person and not as a transaction.

Concentrate on tenure with customer recognition, loyalty programs, needs-based differentiation, customization, and special treatment. "Loyalization" is the goal of obtaining and keeping customers. This is the purpose of the frequent flyer programs. The term "brand loyalty," which is a common expression from the mass marketing discipline, is really a nonsensical idea.

A brand cannot have loyalty. Only a customer can have loyalty. The most loyal customers to Federal Express are those who have lost a package because only then do you see what FedEx does; they bend over backwards to locate the wayward package. They will spend an enormous amount of money and resources tracking down that errant package.

What the typical customer wants, particularly a high-volume purchaser, is a company that recognizes who he is, understands his importance to that company, and helps him solve his own problems or meet his own needs.

Not long ago, only special customers felt entitled to special treatment. But today, the extraordinary is becoming ordinary. What was once a premium – speedy, flawless and responsive service – is now common-place.[11] With dedicated groups, the customers perceive that they are receiving preferential treatment.

From a categorical perspective, some of the best call centers are those that sell things; such centers tend to do a better job than those who service things. Selling call centers have a vested interest and they understand it. So your catalog operations, as a rule, are run much better. They know that if you get put on hold, you are going to hang up and not buy what they are selling. And they know they need to get the order right or you will not call back and buy something else.

The more you can get a customer to communicate with you, the more likely it is that you will be able to a gain a greater share of his business. Inviting that dialogue is becoming the most important creative objective for any company's unsolicited advertising message.

Starting a dialogue with a consumer will be the highest priority for most marketers. Marketing will come to depend more than ever on gaining the customer's trust long enough to begin and sustain that dialogue. The agent can convert any communication opportunity into a potentially valuable cross-selling and problem-resolution opportunity. By asking appropriate questions, the agent can glean valuable information from the customer that can be used to facilitate future opportunities.

Customers do not care about your problems; they care about their own. Dialogue opportunities will provide you with the most useful engagements on which to base further actions, and the most sought-after dialogue should be with the stakeholder who has a complaint.

The Power of the Complaint

In today's atomized business world, the pressure to customize is replacing economies of scale. Niche markets are becoming the whole market. Obviously, no management can afford to give a customer free rein of the factory. Neither can management ignore the slightest soundings from the marketplace, even at the cost of tolerating the annoyances of customers like George Burke.

In the end, a more pragmatic approach to re-engineering the company and increasing dialogue with customers will be utilization of automated systems to absorb the vast "middle" bulk of your dialogue cost burden. This will allow you to pay closer, more labor-intensive attention to the conduct of specialized dialogues at either end of this spectrum. High-value customers are at one end of the spectrum and complainers at the other – complainers who can be converted into ultraloyal collaborators but only through careful, personal attention.

According to the Strategic Planning Study (cited by Tom Peters), about 13 percent of unhappy stakeholders and customers tell 20 other people about their negative experience. If you never hear a complaint, that should be cause for concern and not for self-congratulation. By far the most frequent form of customer feedback is the complaint, and 13 percent of brand switchers change because of complaints that are not handled satisfactorily. The economics of complaint handling can be significant. A successfully resolved complaint will restore potentially lost opportunities and will probably lead to increased business from the complainer.

Computer manufacturer Packard Bell provides an excellent case study.

Woes over quality control have led angry consumers of Packard Bell computers to form on-line chat groups to air grievances. Frustrated users have criticized the company on the WWW; one Web chat room is called "Sad Stories from Packard Bell." Some quoted customers say it has taken an average of three hours to speak with someone. "Don't buy Packard Bell unless you like aggravation," one owner fumed.

Even the company's own dealers, under contract to provide repairs on machines under warranty, sometimes could not get through on the telephone to resolve their complaints. The result was a slowly festering loss of credibility and, most importantly, a declining market share. In one case, a warranty dealer called 23 times over a two-week period trying to order forms to transact business between the two companies. She never did get a response. "It's absurd," she said. "It's never under six phone calls to resolve a problem with them."

In a recent survey by *PC Magazine*, Packard Bell was ranked worst in length of time on hold for customer service (an average of 15.7 minutes). Lack of responsiveness is a sore point with customers. The bottom line is that the negative image with customers is damaging Packard Bell's ability to gain crucial repeat business. Would you want to be a Packard Bell customer right now?

Most large marketing companies, and even smaller ones, have never before been able to identify and capitalize on individual customer dissatisfaction or to detect and prevent individual dissatisfaction and defection. The Internet offers an easily accessible and viperous medium for complaints. A complainer can reach a huge audience on the Internet.

A Note On The Net

The WWW is definitely a model of innovative customer connections and access to products and services. In its current form, the Internet is the closet thing that we have to empowering customers with 24-hour, global access to powerful service applications and reference resources — a form of technology-controlled customer service.

Besides lowering the overhead associated with old labor-intensive methods of service, the Internet unequivocally improves customer satisfaction by giving customers the ability to solve their own problems. What the ATM did for banking in the '80s, the WWW is doing for customer support in the '90s.

Forecasters predict that cybersupport will ultimately become one of the true killer applications of the Internet. Internet-based customer support appeals to stakeholders by offering an expedient alternative to picking up the phone and waiting on hold. Internet customer service access is fast, efficient, interactive, and, most significantly, reduces the load on your service center or help desk. The result is faster answers at lower cost.

Gartner Group surveyed a group of Fortune 100 Chief Information Officers and found that most of them considered on-line customer service the proverbial holy grail of applications. Using the Internet and the WWW, your customers can now access mission-critical customer service and product information at anytime from anywhere in the world. "Customer service is the 'killer app' for the Internet," said Eric Schmidt, CTO, Sun Microsystems.[12]

Conclusion

Companies in nearly all industries will have to contend with faster product cycles, splintered advertising targets, and a fragmented marketplace in which competitive advantage depends upon rapid response to small shifts in consumer needs. Today's mass marketing paradigm has no need for interactive media and computers that track individual customer transactions linked over time.

Martha Rogers argues that any company seeking to profit from the future will need to use technology to become, first, a mass customerizer that efficiently provides individually customerized goods and services and, second, a one-to-one marketer that elicits information from each consumer about his or her specific needs and preferences. The correct combination of the two creates a "learning relationship" – an ongoing connection that becomes smarter as the two interact with each other, thus collaborating to help smart companies keep their customers forever.[13]

Use information about the customer to get more business from that customer. You will be trying to sell a single customer as many products as possible, over a long period of time and across different product lines: preference selling.

Think about all the ways your customers can send information to you. How many ways can these customers actually communicate with you? You can read your mail, of course, but customers are more likely to use a toll-free number or the Internet. On the whole, marketers are more prepared to talk to customers rather than correspond with them.

Because we do not yet live in a world of interactive television, the medium of choice for the future of one-to-one marketing is the telephone. The telephone is the most cost-effective way to reach markets and provide intimate customer service.

Use this technology in the call center to uncover unsuspected selling opportunities and reach stakeholders and prospects in new and highly profitable ways. The most successful companies will build the deepest, most trusting relationships with their customers. Individual, differentiable customer relationships will become the ultimate software of business.

A major shift to telephone marketing and 24-hour electronic customer service is occurring. Call centers play the most important role in this shift because they are the focal point where companies get the closest to the markets that they serve.

The technology and information required to manage millions of such individualized relationships are already available. However, understanding the capabilities of these tools and knowing when and how to use them are not trivial skills. Instead of being overwhelmed by these new tools, you will want more and better tools, more interactivity, more computer memory, and more processing power.

Information technology was a good descriptor 20 years ago when computing and data handling were the end of the story. But now we deploy information technology increasingly to manage various types of relationships: relationships among people, as in call centers; relationships between companies, such as Electronic Data Interchange; and relationships between nations with central bank clearing and settlement networks. Information technology has outgrown its name and has become relationship technology.[14]

The problem is that most call centers have grown up around and with technologies that do not work together. Most banks still have a computer system for every different product they sell. But you cannot be successful in the future as long as your technology is still in the past.

The time has come to shift from the engineering approach of information technology to a human and relationship approach. Instead of product managers, we should develop "relationship" or "customer application" managers. Buy into your customer as a Pareto customer, and give short shrift to those who are less profitable. Dump the deadbeats!

The call center of the "middle-band gap in between" uses call-flow and work-flow systems that are integrated with each other. Both call flow and work flow act as "glue" to make your existing call center applications more effective than they were ever designed to be.

---

[1]Burstein, D. (1995). *Road Warriors*. New York, NY, Dutton-Penguin, 208.
[2]Telemarketing Magazine, Brochure for call center show., Naggi Teherani, Publisher
[3]Burstein, D. (1995). *Road Warriors*. New York, NY, Dutton-Penguin, 87.
[4]Burstein, D. (1995). *Road Warriors*. New York, NY, Dutton-Penguin, 393.
[5]Rogers, M. (1996, Feb. 5). Presentation. Nortel, Dallas.
[6]Burstein, D. (1995). *Road Warriors*. New York, NY, Dutton-Penguin, 108.
[7]Burstein, D. (1995). *Road Warriors*. New York, NY, Dutton-Penguin, 52.
[8]A whole book has been written about this issue, but credit goes to Ed Cavazos, Esq.,

for his newletter and speaking work.

[9]Treacy, M. & Wiersema, F. (1995). *The Discipline of Market Leaders.* Addison-Wesley, Reading, MA. 199.

[10]Petzinger, T. (March 1 1996). "Customer from hell can be a blessing in disguise for sales." *Wall Street Journal*, B1.

[11]Treacy, M. & Wiersema, F. (1995). *The Discipline of Market Leaders.* Addison-Wesley, Reading, MA. 126.

[12]Scopus Technology. (1995). *Scopus WebTeam Brochure,* [Online]. Available FTP: scopus.com.,1.

[13]Pine J., Peppers, D. & Rogers, M. (March-April 1995). Do you want to keep your customers forever? *Harvard Business Review,* inserted supplement. 3.

[14]Bressand, A., and Distler, C. (June 1996). La plane'te relationnelle. *Wired* Magazine, 139.

THE NARROW BAND OF NOW

Paving the Cow Path

Recently, a corporate jet flew into Seattle carrying several important executives. Suddenly, the runway became completely blanketed in fog. The pilot began to circle around, looking for a landmark, but after an hour or so, the plane began to run low on fuel and the passengers became nervous. Finally, a small opening in the clouds appeared and right in the middle was a tall building with one guy working alone on the 25th floor. The pilot banked the plane into a circle, rolled down the window, and yelled to the guy, "Hey! Can you tell me where am I?" The guy in the building yelled back, "You're in an airplane!" The pilot replied, "Thanks." He rolled up the window, executed a perfect 275-degree turn to the north, and proceeded to a flawless blind landing on a dark runway five miles away. Just as the plane pulled to a stop in front of the terminal, the engine ran out of fuel and sputtered to a stop.

The passengers were amazed at the pilot's flying ability and surrounded him to learn how he did it. "Simple," replied the pilot calmly, "I asked that guy in that building a very simple question. And, if you noticed, the answer he gave me was 100 percent correct but absolutely useless. So I knew that must have been the Microsoft Support Center, and from there the airport was right where we found it."

Though this joke embellishes the degree to which we have become 100 percent correct but absolutely useless, its point remains valid. As a culture, we are still in our infancy in applying technology to its most efficient and profitable use. The telephone and the computer are no exceptions. Over the past 150 years, the telephone and the computer have grown as two distinctly different and disparate disciplines. As a result, more enterprises become dependent on automation of technology and do not realize that they are just paving the cowpath.

The recent birth of the microchip has given the PC-based technologies a jump start, while the roots of telephony extend back at least 150 years. Unlike the relatively clean slate of inventions and applications demanded by the digital economy, telecommunication technologies of the past fell often into the rut of not changing the nature of work but simply automating established ways of working.

The problem is that enterprises of today are locked into technologies of the past. These legacy technologies have become super-reliable islands that codify old business practices and old organizational structures. Every dollar spent enlarges the islands rather than bettering them for the future. Because enterprise systems often have a greater lack of vision, enterprises inevitably perpetuate the legacy with each new investment.

A decades-old segregation exists between the data world and the telecom world, and a divergence has grown between them. These two paradigms are the technology of distributed client/server computing and telephony. Cradled in between these two disciplines is the emerging technology of CTI. "Only from the crucible of competition between paradigms can emerge a robust and redemptive new economy of information," wrote one popular futurist.[1]

In the end, CTI may prove that we merely paved the cow path with gold. The time is still too early to tell if CTI is just a fad; if so, it has certainly been a big fad. Forecasters expect CTI software for call centers to swell from a $400 million market in 1996 to a $4.5 billion market in 1999.[2]

The CTI industry is generating more than chump change, even if only a few people besides Harry Newton are making most of the money to be made from it. Later in this chapter I describe an effect called "Newtonization." Unlike most other industries, telephony and call centers in particular have been "Newtonized."

To maintain a client/server LAN environment is no easy or trivial task, much less to implement computer telephony applications, particularly, integrating the rapid prototyping of the Internet. The promise of CTI and its emergence from the call center sector is still mostly unrealized. Companies still lose track of their customers through automation. Like other new electronic commerce substitutes such as the Internet and e-cash, CTI is still relatively untested and will remain an immature discipline into the 21st century.

Many of these new systems have yet to develop the critical mass of participating companies or infrastructure support they need, such as Internet, skills-based routing, and wireless. Many trials are still being conducted. Newtonization may prove ultimately to generate false hope for those who believe that CTI can be as simple as "plug and play" using SoundBlaster Cards. Not only are we tending to pave the cow path with gold but often with CTI as well.

Newtonization

Newtonization \n(y)ü-ten-êye-'za-shen\ n, [fr. *Newton, H.* Am. publisher]: the provocative glamorization of CTI technology that is usually too complex and sophisticated for most of the users who buy it. Newtonization is the fervid amplification of the myth of "plug and play" associated with CTI technology – very much the quintessential technology of customer contact.

Added to considerable hype and a fair amount of confusion among CTI consumers is much dangerous information about the reality of CTI applications. Even Mr. Newton said in 1996 that computer telephony will take time and "will be on everybody's desk in ten years".[3]

The Internet demonstrates this point. Companies are seeking to streamline their call center services via the WWW. Instead they find that the integrations are far more sophisticated than the skill sets of most of the users. These "open" products aren't so open, and do not just drop in. "Plug and play" is in fact "plug and pray." To think that you do not still need people specialized in bridging the chasm between technology fantasy and application reality is unrealistic.

How do we criticize an industry that will grow to more than $4.5 billion in revenues by the turn of the century? Mr. Newton's CT Expo provides an excellent opportunity to understand the pulling of application capabilities by customers and the features pushed by the vendors.

"The barrage of new products released at the Harry show continues, but one key element is missing – the applications. There are plenty of product announcements, alliances, and good intentions coming from the vendors," said one industry analyst.[4]

Products are not quite there yet. In fact, many vendors are still dragging their feet with the introduction of truly open systems. Computer telephony integration is a lot like teen sex: everyone talks about it, few are doing it, and even fewer are doing it right.[5] One of the historically embedded reasons has been the long-standing chasm between the data people and the telecom people.

The Telecom Guys vs. the Data Guys

A gap exists between the data world and the telephony world. Some call it a narrow gap; others call it a chasm, as in *Crossing the Chasm* by Geoffry Moore. On one side, you have call processing with telephone systems and PBXs, managed by telecommunications-oriented people. On the other side, you have the computer systems that handle data processing, generally now referred to as the IS people.

Computer telephone integration lies in the middle area. Data and telecommunications (also called telecom or telephony) are dissimilar, separate worlds using technically diverse products with different interfaces, protocols, standards, languages, and degrees of openness.[6]

Telecom and information systems departments are usually separate and not very often cooperative, although they often office together. The telecommunications manager generally handles the wiring, setup, and maintenance of the phone system. The management information system (MIS) manager has all the applications, databases, and networking.

While the pendulum of purchasing influence swings back and forth between the data and the telecom worlds, the prevailing arc is favoring the telecom. The data world is just now discovering ideas that the telecom people have used for 100 years, and is realizing that they may not be so dumb after all.

Open systems for an open world – standards have existed in the telephone industry for many years, enabling the interoperability of telephone systems around the world. We could certainly argue that phone systems are far more open than computing systems. You can call any other phone system in the world and be connected – from anyplace to anywhere on any other telephone device.

The trend is speeding away from obstructionism, however, by either the data or the telecom people, as interference in most any re-engineering process is becoming a quick and easy career killer.

Look at a larger picture of the cable television industry (heavily influenced by the data world) and the telephone business. The two advantages the telephone companies have over the cable companies are more advanced technology and more money. The phone companies have much greater experience operating the complicated hardware and software necessary for digitally switched networks.

The telecommunications companies such as the Regional Bell Operating Companies (RBOCs) have deployed fiber-optic networks nine times as extensive as those of the cable industry.[7] The interexchange carriers are well financed and have network expertise in fiber optics, wired pair, satellite, and wireless technologies.

Building an interactive system can be justified only if the cable companies can get a piece of the $300 billion telephony revenue stream in the United States. But most companies have a pretty clear idea of what it would cost to rewire North America.

Beware of cable and data people bearing telephony gifts.

The Telecom Guys

Just how far apart are the data and the telecommunications disciplines and their bastard child, CTI?

The more things change the more they stay the same. Computer telephony integration is the perfect example of an option that has been available for years but has never gotten off the ground because the telephony industry could not get the data side of the house to buy in. Neither side wants the other guy's job. Telecom people must take responsibility for the call center's voice mail, which has been poorly implemented, and difficult to maintain and administer in the past.

Even those with a background in data still have an open mind toward voice, but they do not have a foundation in voice. Most people wonder how voice could be all that difficult. Even after the data people took over voice and integrated it into the MIS department, the two sides remained separate because they did not understand each other's business, which they found was not as easy as it looked.

If you have not worked with voice, you do not realize how difficult it can be. My experience is that when the data people are asked to do voice, they do not like to do it any better than the voice people like to do data.

Computer telephony integration is the result of something data people could relate to and embrace. Now, a whole class of standards is emerging that makes data people comfortable with linking everything together and being responsible for it.

Standards such as Telephone Application Programming Interface (TAPI) and Telephone Services Application Programming Interface (TSAPI) offer a neutral area that balances both technologies, enabling them to link together. Standards are coming up and maturing to a practical level that people can really write to and support, and this is what will cause the CTI applications market to explode.

The Data Guys

When it comes to convincing people that they are open, don't let them kid you. Data people are great marketers and self-promoters.

Data people tend to work in open, glass-lined rooms, often with islands set up on raised floors under exquisite lighting. As far back as I can remember, the telecommunications office was usually next to the switch, which was always in a closet under the stairs. I suspect that voyeuristic data people are naturally attracted to the call center business because of the natural fishbowl characteristic of call centers.

Data people are the primary culprits paving the cowpath as a whole, consistently automating business processes that are flawed from the start. What the data people want to do is to connect the PBX as a part of the LAN, like a scanner or a printer. Data people are still focused on developing their distribution networks; telephony is an unnatural act for them.

"Most client/server systems you are building are the wrong systems," information technology pundit James Martin told attendees at the Software and Client/Server World Show and Conference in Toronto during the spring of 1996. They are wrong, he says, because they are automating processes that should not exist in the first place.[8]

Most of the problems with the software data people's building of call centers are that they develop their applications with severe memory bloat that "represents sheer sloppiness." Fat software is faster and cheaper to build. But the call center is the hub of relationship contacts with the customers and, like a heart pacemaker, cannot afford to work only 90 percent of the time.

The biggest beneficiaries of software obesity are the companies that make memory chips. The random access memory (RAM) industry has grown from $1 billion in 1986 to $42 billion in 1995. Intel and Microsoft executives may not actually be conspiring against us, but it sure looks that way. Upgrades are the software industry's version of planned obsolescence.[9]

No technology truly absorbs another. Server-based telephony will find a niche but will not kill the PBX, just as wireless coexists with land lines and radio coexists with television. One reason is because so much of it is out there, a legacy of dead-end technologies.

Managers tend to monitor general traffic flows and adjust the bandwidths on the basis of the unique traffic mix on the network as a whole – watching the forest instead of the trees. Once, analyzing network bandwidth requirements was fairly easy. Now, you have the streams of voice and data, with voice the priority and data being choked out. This explains also the flaw of the Internet phone, the latency, even though a microsecond is enough to annoy most users away in a short time.

North America has more than 60 million Windows users and more than 35 million Novell LAN users. That is a lot of Windows users on Novell LANs. Of all computers, 90 percent use Microsoft software, and 30 million PCs will run Windows '95 during 1996. An irony of the expected success of Microsoft's Window NT and Windows is that when it comes to Internet connectivity, they are awkward systems.

A certain "plug and play" myth among corporations installing personal computers has extended into the realm of telephony. The adroit arrogance of the PC people, such as Microsoft's Charles Fitzgerald, does not wear the mantle of PC-based telephony very well. Industry "Bake Offs" were basically cooking conferences for chefs only – making muffins. Puffery by software companies depends on frequent, expensive upgrades to boost their sales.

Legacy

When asked to describe the main impediments to business process re-engineering, most change managers place legacy technologies high on the list. Such systems tend to be planned in the context of the old systems for production, marketing, financial management, or research. As a result, companies remain saddled with legacy systems that impede rather than catalyze change. The irresistible force of new technology is meeting the immovable object of an estimated $3 trillion installed base of legacy systems.

The problem facing most companies today is that their data usually resides in multiple systems, including accounting, manufacturing, customer support, inventory, and human resource applications. For example, many large companies still use old style, flat-file mainframe databases; while these databases can reliably store a world of bits and bytes, they cannot slice and dice the data.

Tapping legacy databases has been an incredible source of frustration for many companies. A major part of any re-engineering effort is the data conversion. Retaining your current business applications, keeping your databases intact, and continuing to use your present telephone switching system more often than not leads to paving the cow path and automating your mistakes.

The technology legacy is in the tying together of these often disparate systems. Migration in the past has meant that you could only go into multiple databases from different terminals and update with a new release or version, or feature module. You must open each application and make the changes. This is the way of the old legacy, although you can bridge these together to have a single terminal. A company such as NYNEX must pay between $200 million and $300 million a year just to maintain its mainframe software programs, which are often several decades old.

Most of the droves of customer data are largely inaccessible. This problem is not trivial. Many of these legacy islands are old enough to vote and drink. They are not simply "code museums," as some pundits have said. They are operational systems upon which businesses run, so bringing the bulldozer into the data center is not a feasible strategy for fixing the problem.

During the '60s, '70s, and '80s, companies implemented computer systems when the technologies matured to the point where cost-beneficial applications were feasible. Now this equation no longer applies; the company that can understand the migration path of least resistance is the most likely to succeed.

A clean slate in a call center is so rare that most will have to find a graceful way to let go of the past, write it off, and move on without killing what they have bought. Few telecommunications vendors have done exceptionally well at delivering high-quality PBX's with advanced functionality with a clear migration path that can be traversed smoothly without slash-cutting their way out of the legacy burden.

Sometimes PBX technology is viewed as technology of the past, and this perception is deserved because PBX and its more sinister cousin, CTI, often merely automate the old way of working without changing the nature of the work itself. Relative success is often preconceived, much like the VCR, which did not even come close to topping the movie theater businesses as predicted. The predicted death of the PBX simply will not happen in our lifetime.[10]

We have developed in the PBX side of the architecture many capabilities that meet call center requirements. Reliability is one of the best arguments for the longevity of the PBX. We are describing a long, sharp sword where one edge is legacy and the other edge is reliability.

The Clients and Servers of LANs

Client/server systems are clusters of cheap desktop computers attached to a host computer, called a server. They are distributed computing systems that connect programs, applications, servers, and data files that are dispersed over a network of many computers and terminals. Most client/server networks are designed for point-to-point communications between a small number of servers and a large number of clients.

Client/server architecture has taken over the world for several reasons, including the advantages of cheap PC power to the desktop, greater local control, rapid response to changes in requirements, and flexible growth options. In the ideal client/server architecture, the server will be the focal point, or gateway, connecting the various communication and data base resources with a business's stakeholder community. This server is the front end for all the communication technologies used by an organization: e-mail, voice mail, scheduling, project management, on-line, and so on. This server will accept and manage information from many different information-providing back ends, such as voice mail, e-mail, groupware, and the enterprise's ACD. That all of these different information-providing back ends are involved will be completely transparent to the client.

The LANs have certain features that appeal to the telephony world. These include high bandwidth, bandwidth on demand, low-cost standard hardware, shrink-wrapped application software that works on many types of systems, and most importantly, the capability for the users to create and customize reports and the system itself.

The role of the server in the call center will be driven by the need to achieve the following:

- avoid using coding time required on the mainframe
- have servers offload mainframes for better response times
- avoid potential upgrade costs on the mainframe

- provide access to multiple databases on multiple computers
- provide enhanced interface tools
- provide fault tolerance
- disrupt implementations less

Only several companies in the world have any true depth and expertise in the skill set among their people in installing customers' LANs. The recent demonstration by AT&T's lab scientists of one trillion bits transmitted in one second cost tens of millions of dollars to create but shows the upper extremes of network technology available today.

Fiber and fast-cell switching build the new carrier backbones, flexible networks based on a carrier's sophisticated fabric of redundant fiber and ultrafast switches. The efficiency is that I can use different backbones, accomplished by using customers' existing backbones. And although bandwidth allocation techniques are straightforward, based on predictive traffic analysis and possibly some basic queuing theory, if your environment is tightly controlled and is transaction- or batch-oriented, you can build a very accurate model of your traffic patterns.

Experts are needed to make wide area network connectivity work with any degree of reliability. Always ensure that voice has priority over data. Poor-quality video is accepted for videoconferencing but poor-quality audio is not. Is it any surprise that the Wide Area Network experts have emerged from telecommunication companies such as Nortel, AT&T, and a handful of others?

For now though, the issues with wide area network bandwidth are that it is inadequate, overpriced, and often out of reach. The service is hard to price, offerings are difficult to compare, and you can wait forever to get it installed.[11] Concerns about the availability of adequate network management tools will continue to delay widespread implementation of true multimedia systems.

The Failures of Client/Server

Bandwidth concerns are always influential when any CTI application is being implemented. This is not much of a problem so long as applications use the telephone as the client, and the server has a direct connection to the PBX or to an outside phone line (and does not have to send its voice traffic over the network). But if voice traffic is routed over the network as part of an application, understanding bandwidth demands becomes vitally important. Even a small, 15-second voice file requires 1.5 MB of storage.

Server applications tend also to have lengthy implementations, and the reality is that it can take a year or more to move a company off of the mainframe and several more years to iron out the wrinkles. But this is only part of the cost picture. Even as recently as February 26, 1996, *Forbes* writer Lee Sullivan wrote, "It's not unheard of for a new client/server system to be down 30 percent of the time. Client/server architecture has more capability and flexibility, but it comes with a price tag."

The very design of LANs puts them a far distance behind PBX systems in reliability and in their ability to recover from disasters. Failure points include PCs, servers, hubs, LAN hubs, operating systems, databases, and fire walls. Some causes of disk failure are a power surge, a brownout, or a malfunctioning overhead computer.

In a distributed computing system, the failure of one computer, a computer unknown to most other users on the network, can crash and render many others inoperable.

Client/$erver's Costs

There is good news and bad news about CTI in the call center. First, the good news: the migration from mainframe to client/server does not cost a lot of money; after all, you are just replacing mainframes with

Types of disasters requiring computer systems recovery services from 1980 - 1996, based on 228 disasters worldwide.	
Hardware problems	22%
Flood	19%
Power Outage	25%
Other	14%
Hurricane	11%
Fire Explosion	8%
Earthquake	6%
Bomb	5%

inexpensive, powerful PCs.

The bad news is that maintaining client/server-based architectures costs much more than most people think. Client/server systems are becoming cheaper to build but may not be getting cheaper to buy. Contracts for setting up and maintaining client/server systems can cost as much as $5,000 per desktop annually. The Gartner Group Consulting Firm said last year that a client/server system can cost 70 percent more than a mainframe system to maintain. Client/server technology has a high cost to implement and requires the availability of the right products and people to implement and integrate them.

Nevertheless, in the long term, we will find that client/server architectures can be delivered for half the cost of using mainframe architecture. Nobody can say that the old way is better or cheaper.

Choices! Choices! So Many Choices!

I did not create the list on the following page to take up space in the book. I wanted to paint a picture of the multitude of choices facing technology decision makers today. As I began to list all of the technologies and systems that could be found in or related to call centers, I concluded that merely providing the list would make the point. Application managers have to become familiar with different CTI-related technologies and their applications. Is it any wonder that the market is struggling through the integration issues of implementing CTI systems?

CHOICES FACING TECHNOLOGY DECISION MAKERS TODAY

Computers and Servers
Microcomputers
Workstations
Laptops/Notebooks
Pen Based Computers
Applications Servers
E-mail Servers
Data base Servers
Video Servers

CPE Networks
High-speed Ether Net LANs
High-speed Token Ring LANs
LAN Switches
Analog Video Networks
FDDI
ATM
PBX's
Network Controllers

Component Parts
Video Boards
ISDN Boards
Video Cameras
Microphones
Speakers
Modems
Video Codecs
Scanners

System Software
Desktop Operating System
Network Operating System
Multimedia Operating
System
Network Management
Systems

Wide-area Networks
ISDN
Switched 56
T1, T3
Frame Relay
ATM
SMDS

Conferencing Systems
Audioconferencing
Room Videoconferencing
Desktop Videoconferencing
Display Paneling

Semiconductor Chips
Microprocessors
DSPs
ASICs
CCDs

Server OS
Netware
Windows NT
VMS
MVS

UNIX (choose a version)
SCO/Xenix
Sun Solaris
HP/UX
Other

Client Operating Systems
DOS
OS/2
Windows 3.1
Windows 95
Windows NT
UNIX
Macintosh OS

Server Hardware
PC Server
UNIX Workstation
UNIX multiprocessor
VAX/Alpha Chip
Mainframe

**Engineering and Management
Services**
Consulting
Software Development
Systems Engineering
Maintenance

Workflow Applications
FileNet
Recognition/Plexus
Action Technology
Scopus
Answersoft
Aristacom
Staffware
Reach's Workman

Networking
Novell Software
Microsoft Windows NT
Microsoft LAN Manager
UNIX TCP/IP
Remote Dial-in

Groupware Applications
IBM/Lotus Notes
Microsoft Exchange
ICL TeamWare
Novell Groupwise
DEC Linkworks
DEC All-in-1
AT&T Cooperation

Applications Software
Desktop Videoconferencing
Applications Sharing
Whitboard Sharing
E-mail
Group Scheduling
Group Editing
Database Access
Shared Database
Group Document
Management
Work flow Automation
Sales force Automation
Project Management
Graphics

E-mail
Lotus cc:Mail
Lotus Notes Mail
Microsoft Mail
UNIX e-mail
Quickmail
Banyan Intelligent Mail
MCI Mail
Compuserve
AT&T Mail
DEC TeamLinks

119

Computer Telephony Integration

Newtonization and complexity aside, CTI has become large enough and influential enough to command definition as a whole industry, though a relatively small one when you compare it with televisions, cars, or construction. James Burton, a Boston-based consultant in the computer telephony industry, is generally credited with coining the term "computer telephony integration" over 20 years ago. Analysts predict CTI will grow almost 50 percent annually, creating between a $4.5 and $8.0 billion sector of commerce by 1999. This growth has been long in coming.

Computer telephony integration has been around for several decades. Generally, CTI required users to be proficient with and have considerable knowledge about telephone systems as well as networking and database programming to perform even the simplest of tasks.

Historically only large or well-funded call centers could support and develop sophisticated CTI applications. Now, because of the compression of voice into fiber optics and the expansion of chip power to process in real time, CTI is beginning to happen in department size (fewer than 40 agents) call centers, office work groups, individual "knowledge worker" desktops, and the remote hoteling or nomadic office.

Technological elements of CTI include voice processing, telephone network interfaces, touch-tone processing, facsimile, natural language recognition, speaker verification, and text-to-speech. Users of CTI can store, retrieve, and manipulate computer-based information, including voice, over any telephone network. Computer telephony integration is the functional integration of telephone networking capabilities, voice switching, data switching, computer applications and databases, voice processing, and other information media but, most dramatically, of the agents, people, service reps, and knowledge workers.[12]

Five system elements constitute CTI:

- the telephone network, hardware, and services

- the switch, hardware, and software
- the computer, hardware, and software
- a CTI server
- a voice-processing server.

Computer telephony integration is a critical component in the strategic technology of customer contact. Whether customers or stakeholders contact your enterprise through fax, phone, e-mail, or WWW, every interaction should be stored in the same central database of customer and product information. For example, by linking call inquiries to marketing campaigns and sales, the value of any particular marketing or sales project can be determined easily.

By recording and tracking details on every customer input and output throughout the enterprise, a call center solution can leverage the capabilities of CTI into an enterprise customer-relationship management system. Call center managers, in effect, become applications managers, supervising customer interactions and coordinating these interactions across a diverse array of media.

Identifying your callers and the reasons for their calls is the first step in the ongoing process of building and individualizing customer and stakeholder relationships. Each caller is matched to an individualized profile with specific information (buying/purchasing history, contractual status, and preferences) to be used as biographical leverage.

Sometimes CTI gets confused with the benefits it produces. The benefits consist of knowing your customers – knowing when to treat your priority customers with priority and the deadbeats as deadbeats – and being able to identify your opportunities to sell products. Who are your callers, why do they call you, why are they calling you today, and who can best service them during today's call? Answering these questions will help you apply CTI strategies in your call center.

Where CTI really pays off is with transferred calls. Screen pop, also known as intelligent answering, ensures that a telephone call and relevant application data are delivered simultaneously to any agent's desktop. Screen pops dramatically shorten talk time by eliminating the need for data to be reentered. Also, customer data entered by customers, themselves, is more accurate than customer data entered by agents.

CTI Down

For almost 90 percent of companies attempting to implement a CTI application, failure results. However, CTI is not a wasted endeavor for the 10 percent that succeed in a functional integration and use CTI as a stage in a larger re-engineering or reorganization process.

The rising demand for CTI has highlighted several glaring problems with the technology, primarily the lack of bandwidth and standards. Standards are still anything but standard, though they will be required to fully achieve the nirvana of true "plug and play." The more "plug and play" your product offers, the greater your market size will be. As of press time, we had two significant players in the standards arena TSAPI, (Sponsored by Novell, red trunks, in the left corner) and TAPI (sponsored by Microsoft, blue trunks, in the right corner).

The first of these, TSAPI (tee-sappy), is described as a third-party call control that supports advanced features like call monitoring and intelligent call routing. This product is server based and you do not have to add hardware or software to every desktop. Management and administration are centralized. Upgrades to PBXs and even a new PBX are often required.

TSAPI scales well from few to many users but can be expensive for fewer than 100 end users. Because management is centralized, administrative costs are lower. Unfortunately, there are more TSAPI developers than TAPI developers, and they tend to concentrate on corporate and mission-critical features such as interactive voice response, business process automation, and work-flow applications.

The second standard, TAPI, is commonly referred to as support for first-party call control because it allows control of simple telephone functions like dialing, answering, transferring, and conferencing right from the PC on your desk. As TAPI is desktop based, adapters and software must be installed on every PC that needs the TAPI telephone capabilities, although installation is typically simple (plug and play). The PC adapters typically cost $200, but prices are falling rapidly.

TAPI is cheaper for smaller networks (fewer than 100 end users) and most applications are much less expensive than TSAPI. Although TAPI has a large pool of developers, as a whole they do not develop many sophisticated, mission-critical applications.

Many feel that the TAPI/TSAPI rivalry has, to some extent, crippled the CTI industry even as it struggles to exist. In spite of roots going back at least 20 years, only recently was an organization formed to support CTI. Recognizing the rapidly growing market for computer-controlled telephony-based products, the Computer Telephony Resellers Association will once again try to usher in the convergence of two highly evolved disciplines – computer integration and phone systems.[13]

Internet-based CTI applications, such as customer fax-back that allows a LAN to use a single data source for customer phone inquiries, are the type that are pushing LAN-based computer telephony forward. And applications focusing on groupware integration are also adding new dimensions to CTI. Unfortunately, the failures of implementing success-ful computer telephony applications are more a result of the way the technology was used than of the technology, itself. Most often, the technology has simply automated the old way of doing things.

In and of itself, CTI may be a wonderful technology; however some of the parasitic baggage that it supports is sure proof that our cultural evolution will not keep pace with the technical evolution. With CTI comes all of the frequently misinterpreted equipment and costs associated with operating a client/server system architecture. ISDN is one such cramp.

Integrated Services Digital Network

The RBOCs' research arm, Bell Labs, developed ISDN technology a decade ago, but RBOCs got serious about marketing it only recently. The result of years in which hundreds of millions of dollars were invested globally by the telephone companies has resulted in a completely digital backbone. ISDN is one of the speedy, high-capacity services to emerge from this comprehensive and sweeping decades-old upgrade and overhaul of the public phone network.

Unlike ordinary analog telephone service, ISDN gives users a completely digital end-to-end connection, allowing for speedy data connections among branch locations. ISDN keeps the data in digital form from end to end and moves text at a rate of 128 Kbps per second. ISDN's rapid data transfer rate can be 10 times faster than ordinary modem connections. These faster rates come in handy for those who want to browse the graphic-intensive Internet at twice the usual speeds of typical modems. The fastest modems available communicate at 28.8 Kbps per second, or roughly a page of text every second.

Because ISDN is a completely digital connection, it requires no set-up time, an advantage for remote agents, telecommuters, and out-of-office workers who need remote access to corporate computer networks.

Dataquest predicts that the number of ISDN lines will double to one-half million in 1996 and will hit 2.2 million by the end of the decade. In 70 percent of the United States, ISDN is expected to be available by the end of 1996. Pacific Bell is already up to 80 percent coverage, and NYNEX, to 46 percent. In many cities, ISDN is affordable with the service costing between $30 and $60 per month. One strength of the large telephone companies is that they can bring the Internet to consumers through ISDN because their core skills are so closely related.

As for servicing and installing the ISDN base, unfortunately, the telephone companies have become just about as reliable as the cable companies. The RBOCs have long been derided for their spotty service at delivering advanced data services, and ISDN proves it. The amount of hidden costs, misinformation, and lack of support makes ISDN still a questionable technology at best.

The real problem is telling your phone company how to provision your ISDN line and providing it with the exact details on a dozen obscure parameters to install your line. Many central offices have analog equipment and cannot use ISDN. Half of the country still cannot get it. Even if you are entitled to order the service, you will probably have to suffer through several phone company order-takers before you find one who knows what you are talking about. Although ISDN is supposed to be a standardized service, it has subtle local variations. Expect that you and the phone company will have to tinker with your respective phone lines before the connection works.[14] Furthermore, your Internet service provider may not have ISDN on its end of the line.

Integrated Services Digital Network is not cheap, especially when you concede that an ISDN modem costs about $500. However, higher speed T1 lines at 1.54 megabits per second can cost $1,000 per month or more. Once connected to the Central Office, you are often still constrained to the 64 channels of the T carrier and Sonet systems that transmit signals between telephone central offices. Phone companies say that prices are high because the technology is extraordinarily expensive.[15]

So why is ISDN not as popular as cable TV? With the advent of the Internet and its graphic-based content, local phone companies are pushing ISDN, which only offers data rates as high as 128 Kps. But at 128 kilobits-per-second speeds, ISDN provides a picture quality inferior to normal television.

Integrated Services Digital Network is too slow for the requirements of newer advanced multimedia capabilities that on-line services, Web pages, and industrial applications demand. You certainly wouldn't want a doctor to operate on you remotely guiding an ISDN-based robot.

Slowly, ISDN is being buried by the unrealized threat of DSL services and their even faster progeny, Very high-bit-rate Digital Subscriber Line (VDSL) service. Compared to these emerging transmission schemes, ISDN's 128 Kps do not seem very fast anymore.

Because ISDN is digital, you cannot just pick up the line and have a dial tone indicate it is working. This may be the biggest leap of faith for everyone who grew up accustomed to hearing the sound of a dial tone.

After two decades of being mocked initially as "Innovation Subscribers Don't Need" and progressing to "It Seems Do-able Now," ISDN has basically ended up as an "I Still Don't kNow" type of service. A middle-band service that will never emerge as the holy grail of the Internet, ISDN is still too slow. It survives because it services the middle ground between traditional modems and T1 speeds. But the telephone companies know that ISDN is a dead language, although they may not want to admit it.

The telephone companies are putting the brakes on the deployment of ISDN by keeping prices and complexity artificially high because they know that ISDN is already outdated. Critics say also that ISDN pricing is beyond the reach of most consumers. This service requires expensive hardware and software modifications that have technical glitches. This resistance and its bandwidth inferiority makes ISDN a serious contributor of poop on the cow path.

Frame Relay

Frame relay is the big bandwidth equivalent to ISDN, although, like ISDN it is enormously popular despite its shortcomings. Frame relay was

126

designed strictly as a data service with, initially, no provision to support time-sensitive traffic like voice or data linked with voice in multimedia applications (follow-me data).

Weeks or even months can be required to become provisioned, with massive coordination delays between local service providers and national carriers always compounding expected problems.

Voice conversation needs less than 200 milliseconds of network delay for any type of quality, and some people detect a discernable delay with half that amount. The central problem with frame relay is one of delay, compounded by wild variances. Often – and spontaneously – a voice will burst off and sound like an inebriated Swedish sailor cursing the weather over a static-filled CB radio.

To address this problem, some frame relay service providers are beginning to offer priority service contracts and some carry service guarantees. Voice to the frame relay people is simply another type of data stream, and you must monitor voice quality and latency levels closely. If you can get by with low latency from your carrier, voice over frame relay can save you big money.

Frame relay is not the best service to use in the call center environment. In an environment where 100 percent reliability is absolutely required, negotiating for quality of service guarantees makes no sense.

Fax Faux Pas Will Be Passé

When a large retail catalog operation began to offer a fax number along with other forms for ordering, the number of transmissions began to grow at a rapid rate. Most of their voice calls were placed after normal business hours, when customers were at home, and the fax orders came in during the business day. This led the retailer to believe that people were using fax machines where they worked. In time they became surprised at the dramatic shift in order-arrival patterns that lessened the human agent staffing problems.

The facsimile will be judged in retrospect as having been a step backward; its ramifications will be felt for a long time. This condemnation appears to fly in the face of a telecommunications medium that has seemingly revolutionized the way we conduct our business and, increasingly, our personal lives. But people do not understand the long-term cost and the short-term failings of the fax. We can point to the Japanese for this singularity.

As recently as 10 years ago, Japanese business was conducted not by documents but by voice, usually face to face. Few Japanese businessmen had secretaries, and correspondence was often painstakingly handwritten in a pictographic Kanji. A single Kanji symbol out of a total of more than 60,000 made the fax a natural device to use. Their culture, language, and business customs are very image oriented. Since little Japanese was then in computer-readable form, few disadvantages arose.

The fax is a Japanese legacy, but only because they were smart enough to standardize and manufacture them better than anybody else, just as they did with VCRs. For computer readability of a language as simplistic as English, with the 26 letters of the Latin alphabet, 10 digits, and a handful of special characters, thinking in terms of 8-bit ASCII is much more natural.

Western Union's automatic telegraph (1883) was hard-wired, point-to-point e-mail. The general use of e-mail as we know it today, multipoint to multipoint, predates the general use of fax. When e-mail started during the middle and late '60s, relatively few people were computer literate. Therefore, that e-mail was overtaken by fax in the '80s is not surprising.

Most contemporary fax machines conform to a set of standards, known as group 111. Group 111 standards establish digital image-scanning and data-compression rates. Machines built to this standard can transmit data at a maximum 9,600 bits per second, tops. Because of this digital speed ceiling, fax is not even economical to use anymore.

One page of this book would take about 20 seconds (about 200,000 bits of information) to send by normal fax at 9600 baud. Even so, by the early '90s, fax transmission had become the preferred method for rapidly sending printed material.

Most business letters today are prepared on a word processor, printed out, and faxed. Think about that! We prepare our document in such computer-readable form that we think nothing about passing a spell checker over the words.

Anybody who has tried to use a rent-a-fax machine in an airport or airplane knows that faxes get sent over garbled, backed up phone lines (most planes only have four to eight lines that overload quickly). These machines are expensive to use, cost more than $3 per minute, and create obnoxious unexplained credit card rejections and poor and inaccurate billing for calls that never go through.

The way fax-on-demand works for most call centers is the agent asks the caller to "please call our fax-on-demand number at . . . ," while in reality the agent is thinking, "I've only said this a thousand times." The problem is that call centers are designed to handle dialogue and conversations; fax (and IVR) usually "grow up" around the call center in an ad hoc fashion. The fax machine forms a serious blemish on the information landscape, a dead-end exit off the information superhighway, and will prove to have been a rather large pothole on the cow path.

Skills-based Routing

Computer telephony integration, the technological basis for a popular call center application called skills-based routing, permits call transaction types to be identified, even before being answered in some approaches, and routed to only that subset of agents trained to deal with that kind of transaction. Picking up where hunt groups left off, skills-based routing allows callers to be identified by various information sources and then routed to the most skilled agent available for the immediate task.

The thinking here is that by offering transaction types only to those agents skilled in that transaction, average talk time will decrease and quality will improve. In theory, this will eliminate all ACD microqueue management issues and associated overhead costs.[16]

Theoretically, the assumption is good. But skills-based routing and the CTI technologies that it is based on seem to be getting out of hand. Many call centers attempt blindly to develop elaborate skill inventories for their agents and then find themselves unexpectedly administering incredibly complicated application matrices embedded in skills-based routing schemes. Conceptualized around mid-1995, skills-based routing is a highly complex interaction of variables with a dark side that has only now emerged.

Many of these efforts may result in potentially bad long-term consequences: overworked skilled agents; queue management and load imbalances; varying skill sets present (often changes daily); external forces (e.g. weather layoffs); scheduling issues; and added complexities. Skills-based routing efforts also change skill levels, and changes that must often be tied to compensation tracking – the more skills you have, the more you get paid, but only if you are taking calls for those skills.

Another problem with skills-based routing is acute agent specialization, which in fact results in longer queue times. Agent specialization may make some short-term sense but appears to have undesirable long-term consequences.

Skills-based routing is a double-edged sword and requires a stalwart rethinking of the call center. A consistent, ongoing administrative effort is required to keep the skills database up to date, including customer needs lists and other routing tables.

A Final Word on CTI

Two factors affect the success of any CTI project: the availability of technical expertise, and training and agent support. The agent base can subtly sabotage a project if attitudes are not kept in check. Agents must buy into the benefits of CTI to the degree that they promote the implementation themselves.

Standards such as TSAPI and TAPI are making CTI available to the smaller and informal call centers that could not previously afford CTI capabilities. The overriding mission of CTI is to give the customer more control without regard to whether he is PC-centric or phone-centric. The merging of these disciplines will create opportunities that will help businesses regain control over their telecom infrastructure, integrating a CTI infrastructure with customer-centric information-tracking applications.

How well CTI-based applications work and how far they will extend will depend on how well these links are built. All the pieces of the CTI puzzle are out there, but no unified channel exists through which the product can flow. For the most part, companies hoping to spin gold out of the ether of the cybersphere are contributing to paving the cowpath with that gold using CTI.

Even advocates of the wireless say that the CTI industry is embryonic, and analysts say that CTI applications are anything but mature. Bartholomew Stanco, of Gartner Group in Stanford, Massachusetts, asserts that, "By no means is CTI plug and play."

For the short term, CTI is still being defined. Some even argue that CTI is becoming less important because we have built all the standard interfaces into our products, across all the platforms.

CTI is and will be a morph in progress for the next 15 years. In fact, the morph of computer and telephone is still a picture of two separate entities not truly merged. Intelligent, networked-based CTI will be the next generational development from CTI technologies. Delivering useful CTI-based programs through the Internet and for corporate intranets will be one of the next big areas of growth.

The call center is where the Internet is having to prove its worth. Unlike the use of corporate *intranets*, the Internet as an ACD bypass will become important but will never entirely replace the telephone as an ideal means of communication. The Internet does carry a considerable amount of information, but very little of that information is voice – the seminal foundation of call centers.

The Internet: the Good, the Bad, and the Ugly

As pragmatists for the most part, those who are involved in the technologies of customer contact can do little to escape the frenzied and pervasive expectations for the Internet. Call center technologists should understand the good, the bad, and the ugly of the Internet because, although relatively little activity integrating the Internet to the call center has occurred, half-assed integrations (acceptable to Internet digit-heads but not to call center managers) are the rule. Call centers may be the last place we see Internet integration, but the Internet will certainly survive in one form or another for a long time.

The Internet buzzed for two decades before becoming an overnight sensation. Before WWW, the Internet was a specialized network for government and academic institutions; today, it is almost a centerpiece for popular culture, individuals, and businesses.[17]

One year's worth of Internet traffic represents more words than have been published through traditional means through all the history of human writing. The Internet has surpassed the U.S. Post Office as a carrier of mail; one comparison estimates 1 trillion e-mail messages delivered while there were only 180 billion postal deliveries. The Internet now transports more digital data bits than the total number of voice bits over the telephone system.

Vinton Cerf, senior vice president of data architecture at MCI and codeveloper of the computer networking protocol used by the Internet (Transfer Control Protocol/Internet Protocol) predicts the existence of 1.6 million networks by the year 2000. Traffic on the Internet is estimated to be expanding about 300 percent per year!

Although 40 percent of all Internet traffic originates currently from Southern California, more than 50 percent of Internet users are outside of the United States, and that percentage is rising. By the year 2000, U.S. users should account for less than 20 percent.

Home use of the WWW section of the Internet doubled between July 1995 and January 1996 but still represents only 8 percent (about 7.5 million) of U.S. households. Estimates of home and office use of the WWW use reach as high as 17.6 million people.[18] Demographics show a preponderance of primarily young, white, and well-educated male users.

Growth in U.S. Consumers with Internet access:

1994	5 million
1995	10 million
1996	17 million
1997	22 million
1998	32 million

Growth in pages of information on the WWW:

1994	6 million
1995	6 million
1996	6.5 million
1997	11 million
1998	26 million

The Internet is expected to account for 40 percent of all business transactions over the next 10 years. The prevailing vision is that the Internet will become a giant catalog with as much impact as the billions in revenues and customer interactions that the mail order catalog and junk mail industries have generated.

The cyberdream is to allow customers to use WWW browsers instead of the telephone for information and service exchange. Many people have long envisioned the Internet as a massive electronic mall in the making – a place where people could buy and sell on-line 24 hours a day.

And yet, in early 1996, the returns remain less than inspiring. Most of the estimated 17.6 million people who use the Internet are not buying or selling anything. What most Internet users are doing is trading information that is useful in their everyday lives.

Take launching a catalog business on the Internet, for example. A CD demo of the catalog is created and is sensational, with inviting Web pages contained full-screened, sensual speaking women inviting you to order. But how does this demo look at ISDN speeds? The cybermodel shrinks to a window the size of an index card and the sensual voice grows shrill and rough. The pages no longer speedily burst out on demand, and you are back to frustratingly long connection and download times. So much for the consumer's instant gratification and impulse purchase habits.

The most significant influence on the (lack of) growth of Internet shopping is that other more mature, viable commercial alternatives exist already. For example, six times a year I get a colorful printed catalog delivered to my mailbox. This catalog is portable, easy to carry around, to bookmark, to annotate, and to dog-ear the pages for future reference.

Retail demographics of the Net show that if your product is sold primarily to women, you can anticipate not generating much revenue from the Internet. (Only 29 percent of Internet users are female, according to a Georgia Tech Survey).

Male/female demographics aside, an October 1995 survey of Internet users, conducted by the Georgia Institute of Technology's College of Computing, found that only 11.1 percent of 23,000 respondents claimed to shop on the Internet, while 51.8 percent said they use it for work and 63.3 percent, for entertainment. Sixty percent of those surveyed cited security as the primary reason for not buying on the Internet.[19]

Shopping without sales clerks is an uncultural thing to do in North America, and change is difficult. People are not accustomed to buying on the Internet yet because of the credit card security issue, although the Internet is currently capable of engaging in secure financial transactions. This issue is no longer technical but merely cultural.

The slow acceptance of Internet business may come also from the nature of the market rather than from problems with the technology. Right now, the Internet appears to have more prophets than profits.

In fact, today's technologies and delivery vehicles satisfy many retail consumers well enough that the benefits of moving to electronic-based commerce cannot be justified by the limitations of conventional stores and catalogs.

Technology pundits say they would not be surprised to see electronic mail take a backseat to more mundane tasks. Early radio pioneers made the mistake of predicting that radio would serve chiefly as a device for broadcasting the names and addresses of businesses – with music as filler in between ads. The real users of the technology are more the inventors than the promoters. All communications services are unpredictable because they will be driven by what people want to do with them. The Web has a lot to offer, but not what you think.[20]

Eric Schmidt, CTO of Sun MicroSystems, says that as far as the Internet is concerned, "customer service is [will be] the 'killer app' for the Internet . . .," not consumer retailing.[21] In a survey of Fortune 2000 CIOs, the Gartner Group found that most considered on-line-supported customer service the proverbial holy grail of applications.

Several serious issues are related to making the Internet viable commercially: the severity of financial transactions, lack of a direct response mechanism, and a difficult user interaction. Customers who are being told to combine Internet technologies with the company's other financial services and collections retain a healthy skepticism.

Once a safety net is in place, Internet call centers will be as fundamental as phone-based call centers. This safety net encompasses both technical needs (transaction security) and sociological needs (my wife says, "I'm going shopping, I don't know what for – I'm just mall surfing"). As an ACD bypass, the Internet will remain relatively immature for several more years. For most, the visibility of being accessible from the Internet will offer much greater advantages than the revenues it will generate.

The Good

The Internet is an ACD bypass method that allows customers 24-hour, worldwide access to mission-critical customer service and product information. In the ideal model of the Internet, every field technician, salesperson, executive, and call center agent has access to the same valuable information and powerful problem-resolution facilities.

New software lets individuals access information on host and legacy systems. For example, retrieving bank account information with Hyper Text Markup Language compatible browsers is comparable to transactions typically accomplished over the phone. From this philosophy of link-happy call center applications came the Internet-based applications.

Regarding Internet-based ACD applications, voice over the Internet should be distinguished from Internet access to the call center. The information-access application typifies the call flow we will see more commonly for at least several more years:

- The caller activates a "call me" kick plate, radio button from any Web page.
- The Internet home page sends request to an "Internet response unit" (IRU).
- The IRU formats the message into ACD call command.

- The ACD blends in predictively to call-flow schedule the call, either immediately or in the future.
- The ACD then dials the user's phone number.
- On answer, the ACD connects an outbound service agent to the caller.

Reduced agent talk time is a significant benefit of a properly implemented Internet call center interface. An agent knows exactly (the caller decided from the Web page) what to discuss with the caller before the call is connected. Similarly, if a customer accesses a company's WWW site to obtain technical support, his name and telephone number can be collected, stored, and queued into a predictive dialing application for an outbound proactive problem-resolution campaign. Even a call-back request can be queued and routed, based on the business rules, skills matrices, requested call back times, and specific escalation procedures.

This type of "call me" kick plate Internet/ACD application differs substantially from that envisioned by the proponents of the Internet phone technology. Whereas the practical limits of the Internet and ACD integration are marked by the "call me" kick plates, Internet idealists (the ones who get that glazed, wired, hypnotic look) see the Internet soon supporting reliable voice calls as well as faxes and full-motion video, in spite of the fact that the first really commercially viable Internet phone only hit the market in spring 1995.

The immediate viability of the Internet phone is driven only by the economics of the long-distance telephone market, where international calls can run up to $120 per hour. An Internet-based phone could make the equivalent call for as little as $6 per hour.

The big problem is that the transmission delay is still there, and, even in full-duplex conversations, Internet telephony, with all of its hang-ups, isn't quite ready to revolutionize telecommunications. A $6-an-hour international call may be enough to justify fuzzy, jumpy, static-filled connections, but it certainly wouldn't fly with a customer calling to place an order with your company. The bandwidth problems that mark the rest of the Internet also depress Internet telephony quality – a prime reason why telephone companies are not sweating bullets over the threat of Internet telephony.

The Bad

According to a study by O'Reilly & Associates, 98 percent of Americans do not have access to the Internet.[22] Most non-Internet users would not find anything they really want as the Internet is described consistently as having 500,000 channels and nothing to watch. Content providers everywhere have been throwing heaps of "content" (marketing spam) onto the Web just to see what sticks. The result is largely garbage. For example, Playboy's and Penthouse's Web pages are extremely popular sites, and until more publishers start putting up content to compete with naked ladies, the Internet's reputation as a portal for pornography will undoubtedly remain secure.[23]

The Web currently has few videos and huge multimedia offerings that users see in real time anyway. Simple mathematics explains why: of all of the Web users in 1996, some 13.4 million people will dial up using regular modems, only 900,000 will use cable modems in 1996, and almost all of these will be trial users of the technology.[24] Because the local phone companies have a lock on the "final mile" – the wiring that reaches into the home – the maximum speeds available for most users is 28,800 bps. And while the popular press glamorizes the transportation of megabytes, almost-megabyte systems are on campuses and in large companies, where only kilobytes are available in the suburbs.

Years of monopoly have left the local phone companies with outdated networks, ill-suited to the new generation of bit-hungry and transaction-happy Net users. Surfing the Internet has left many surfers facing a busy signal until a line opens up. Also, the Internet remains a difficult environment for neophytes to navigate. But this will change rapidly in the next several years, mostly through the efforts of the telecommunications giants like Nortel, the baby Bells, and AT&T.

AT&T has had several fits and starts in the on-line wars and is not the only company chasing Internet revenue. Sprint is the largest carrier of Internet traffic, and MCI has just announced its combined efforts with Microsoft. The baby Bells, which already claim most of the phone customers in the United States, are readying their own mass distribution Internet access systems. The precursor to completely integrated call center-Internet access will come from the baby Bells and the large Internet service providers that are already discussing strategies and processes to support millions of users through call centers. In a rare breath of sanity, they are not kidding themselves either. Servicing a computer inquiry is much more complicated than handling complaints about phone service or a credit card bill.[25]

The Internet is growing through the addition of routers, specialized computers that read, address, and send information packets on their way. A single Web page may have to go through as many as 20 routers to reach its destination, your customer's PC. In the last several years, Internet traffic has taken on more GIFs (Graphic Internet Files), doubling the number of bits every couple of months. With the growth of graphic-based content, 28,800 bps speed of dial-up access available to most people seems almost Jurassic, even though it approaches the maximum limit of today's network.

As the Internet veers toward its preordained impact with television and telephony as the primary source of information, entertainment, and communication for the public, the prime obstacle is bandwidth. In its current form, the Internet will not support broadband services of the type the consuming masses are expecting. If you tried to connect a broadband modem to the Internet, you would have a ridiculous impedance, a mismatched bunch of firehoses attached to a network of garden hoses. Bottom line: for the foreseeable future, on-line services will bog down in slow accesses, sticky searches, jerky movements, and blurred faces.[26]

The Ugly

The biggest fear now is watching the Internet bog down under an increasing gluttony of graphics – "GIF-raft" and traffic jams. This causes the Internet's brownouts, in which response time becomes intolerably slow. More than once has most of the California Internet traffic, the source for two fifths of its total traffic, experienced brownouts when it suffocated PacBell's ATM switches.

During 1995, users of the WWW reported several brownouts, when communication on the Internet was impossible or ridiculously slowed. These delays have been attributed to various factors including software errors, excessive traffic, and overload of simultaneous Web servers. Most often a combination of these elements creates brownouts. As these networks expand worldwide, expect more brownouts.[27]

Cataclysmic brownouts to the North American telephone network are not uncommon and began before 1990. In January 1990, the AT&T long-distance network experienced a large-scale brownout that lasted for nine hours; 60,000 people lost all service and 70 million calls could not be completed. The failure was attributed ultimately to a software bug that caused a backup switch to fail after the main switch failed. More recently, a massive power failure of the Pacific Northwest's power grid paralyzed the Northwest in July 1996.

Depending on whom you talk to, the data in as few as 12 to 100 full-motion videos could bring the Internet to its knees. Increasingly, experts predict the collapse of the Internet in 1997. To a spring 1996 ComNet plenary session audience, networking guru Robert Metcalf said that the worldwide network would recover from a collapse such as this, but that irresistible and irrevocable forces are at work to bring it down. Among them are the insufficient capacity of the local loop and backbones, breaking of the "compatibility platform," lack of security and effective "digital money," and the economic fact that more money is pouring into the Internet than is pouring out.[28]

The Internet has speed wobble, and nobody is managing it. Anything totally unmanaged is likely to get out of hand, growing catastrophically and engaging in wild gyrations of growth somewhat similar to the ride of a wild stock market (look at the billion dollar star of Netscape).

Not everyone will agree with me on this, and most of my critics will beat me up on it. However, I cannot evangelize something so inherently flawed as the Internet in its current form, particularly since its very nature is setting it up for the experience of cataclysmic change. As cutting edge as call centers are, I doubt that the pragmatic nature of those responsible for managing their customer and stakeholder contact technologies will allow them to jump on the bandwagon of something so volatile and unpredictable as the Internet.

Already the explosion of Internet use has demonstrated the shortcomings of the phone system as the on-line crowds log in. To keep the Internet users from knocking the voice traffic off of their networks, all of the phone companies are spending hundreds of millions of dollars upgrading their switches and lines. Phone companies see ATM as the salvation of their bandwidth requirements.

Some good will come of the impending Internet overload. The Phoenix rising from the ashes will be asynchronous transfer mode. The emergence of asynchronous transfer mode will happen by calamity when the Net crashes and users demand, or pay for, broadband services. Asynchronous transfer mode will be the backbone of that new network, extending near unlimited bandwidth to the desktop with fiber optics.

Internet Forecast

The problems with the Internet in its current form may be insurmountable. Addresses may be insufficient, routing is inadequate, traffic is too heavy, domain names are excessive, contentions for domain names are increasing, expense is too great, and measurable returns are too little. The specter of increased regulation threatens the very survival of the Internet.

The Internet is essentially very slow, so the idea of its ever being the primary multimedia hookup in the home is sheer nonsense.[29] Furthermore, today's residentially available low-speed, low-bandwidth PC networks such as the Internet need upgrading before they can offer high-quality interactive multimedia and video services such as the Jetsons and Spock enjoy.

Using the Internet does offer an intriguing opportunity in the area of customer service and support for high-tech products. Many predict that on-line customer service will be the next "killer app" of the Internet. In time, that point of convergence will move out of the call center right to the customer's desk, where the real power is. Customers will use applications like the Web page on demand to open their own trouble tickets, check status, research databases, and, most importantly, demand service.[30]

The answer to traffic jams on a narrow band Internet is simple: create a broadband Internet. A vastly different Internet emerges when it is delivered at the 1.5 million bits per second that is T1 or ADSL and faster, such as cable modems. With all of the bandwidth at our fingertips, the WWW should soon cease to be a novelty and solidify its foundation for interactive commerce and entertainment. Experiences will change radically when you can access TV-quality video and download stuff from the world's 5 million Web servers nearly as fast as you can open a file on your hard drive.

Most of the long-distance carriers are moving to market the Internet as a phone like consumer service. MCI plans to increase the capacity of its network systems to handle an expected boost in traffic from new individual consumers. The marketing-savvy long-distance companies are trying to woo consumers with aggressive, flat-rate pricing plans that smaller competitors will be hard-pressed to beat. The entrance by the long-distance carriers may be absorbing a confusing array of phonelike discount plans to the Internet market.[31]

The Internet is a major force for most companies. If they are not connected, they lack a perceived way to provide service to their customers. The Internet will be, eventually, a force to be reckoned with. Its impact on the way we will provide and conduct business is, and will be, undeniably significant. But right now, the Internet remains a great model but a lousy method. The Internet is not moving from a promising social experiment to a slick, electronic shopping mall as quickly as expected. We are just waiting for the Web to grow up.

Immature technology has no place in the call center. Combined use of the Internet and call centers is so new that only as recently as March 1995 was the first patent for Internet connectivity to an ACD issued. In September 1995, the first commercial Internet ACD application was demonstrated between Cooperative Marketing Concepts and The Sharper Image. The Internet represents another nonstandard way of ordering, but will remain a niche customer contact form, an important form of integrated ACD bypass.

At this point, dabbling in the Internet is where most call center technologists should be, but I wouldn't spend huge capital investments on Internet connectivity until both the Internet and the technologies required to interface the call center with your stakeholders and customers mature.

Many profits will be gained from the Internet, and the proper blending of directly assisting Internet browsers, users, and customers will increase sales and satisfaction. The only thing that matters is that the applications work the way your organization intends, but most of them are simply not designed to be distributed over vast geographic areas, and providing the required bandwidth can still be extraordinarily expensive. Are you prepared to handle and respond to Internet inquiries from Japan or Holland?

Conclusion

Changes in customer habits are an indication of increasing consumer demand for CTI. In the groupware world of Lotus Notes, for example, about 97 percent of users carry notebook computers. Approximately 75 percent of all users also carry cellular phones compared with the previous year, 1995, when only 40 percent carried cellular phones. One-way beepers and two-way pagers are experiencing the same type of growth. Last year, between 30 percent and 40 percent of Notes users, and now 70 percent, also carry pagers. If people are carrying all three, they want to be accessible and access services in a number of different ways.[32]

In a 1996 study by Deloitte & Touche's Consulting Group, ACDs and advanced call centers were used in 56 percent of the respondents' environments, including a whopping 88 percent of the retail sector. Pagers, cellular phones, and the Internet are just examples of the impending integration requirements of customer and stakeholder contact. We will see broad connectivity available on business desktops much sooner than we see it available to most people in their homes.

The secret to customer contact technologies lies in integrating single, centralized databases that track details on each and every contact made by marketing, sales, support, and call center agents with their customers and stakeholders. The technologies used to identify the calling behavior of "most valued customers" should not be overlooked. Successful technology integration requires that all agents have access to the same central knowledge base of customer and product information, whether they interface remotely through the Internet or through a networked computer LAN, or even through wireless modems.

The technologies of customer service are evolving out of the narrow band and into a middle band, characterized by interactive, work-flow and call-flow regulated, type-based chats, two-way screen pops, and audio conversations through not just the dial phone but through the Internet, faxes, and cellular phones. Narrow-band technologies are a poor driver of productivity. Corporations must rethink their applications and the technology that they are based on as distribution of applications, products, and services across greater distances increases.

The key to solving this problem is for business leaders to define a target architecture for information technology and to devise a migration path to achieve it. Profiting from CTI-based applications requires not only digital bandwidth but broad-minded thinking about how to use and implement (and rapidly change) applications to suit our stakeholders. The rapid maturing of technology standards now makes it possible to plan an entire enterprise architecture rather than just adding another "room onto the farmhouse."

Today's merging – not emerging – technology is a natural evolutionary requisite to achieving the eagerly sought full-motion interactive video on demand: video dial tone. Getting there poses an interesting challenge. How do companies create the conditions that allow new investments to contribute to a desired future rather than perpetuate and pave the cowpaths of the past? Knowing and understanding the broadband technologies of tomorrow are certainly critical. Once you have a vision of how your stakeholders will engage you, the challenge becomes either to integrate or to die.

Integrate with what? Understanding the broadband devices of tomorrow will give technologists, particularly those who need to remain grounded in the reliable technologies of customer contact, an advantage that those blinded by cyberhype do not enjoy.

---

[1]Gilder, G. (Feb. 26,1996). Telecosm. *Forbes ASAP*,101.

[2]Robinson, T., (July 8, 1996) Wake-Up Call, *Communications Week*, 41.
[3]Newton, H. (March 14,1996). CTI Expo notes.
[4]Semilof, M. (March 11,1996). The promise of CTI is still unrealized. *Communications Week*, 37.
[5]Pabon, R. (March 13,1996). Bosch Telecom CTI Expo presentation notes.
[6]ibid. 104-10.
[6]Woods, L. (Feb. 27,1996). Plane calls still miss connection. *Wall Street Journal*, B1.
[6]Burstein, D. (1995). *Road Warriors*. New York, NY. Dutton-Penguin, 200.
[6]VanDoren, D. (Feb.12,1996) Vangaurd Communications presentation notes, Washington, D.C.
ibid.
[7]Burstein, D. (1995). *Road Warriors*. New York, NY, Dutton-Penguin. 440.
[8]Source: Client Server World, April 12, 1996, Grant Buckler
[9]Kichen, S. & Sullivan, L. (Feb. 26,1996). *Forbes Computers/Communications*, 104-110.
[10]Geng, K. (Feb. 13, 1996). Keynote speech BCR PBX96 Conference, Seimans Rolm.
[11]Willis, D. (April 23,1996). Inadequate, overpriced bandwidth clouds the condition of the WAN, State of the WAN, 6.
[12]VanDoren, D. (Feb. 12,1996). Vanguard Communications presentation notes, Washington, D.C.
[13]Henderson, T. (April 2,1996). PR Newswire,
[14]Shaffer, R. (Nov. 6,1995). Speed freaks: try ISDN now. *Forbes*, 348.
[15]Woods, L. (Feb. 27,1996). Plane calls still miss connection. *Wall Street Journal*, B1.
[16]Scopus Technology. (1995). Scopus WebTeam Brochure, [Online]. Available FTP: scopus.com, 2.
[17]Simone, J. (March, 1996). ATM-the business case. The ATM Internet, 5-6.
[18](March 7, 1996,). WWW home use doubled in 2nd half of '95. Wall Street Journal, 4.
[19]Source: Ted Doty, NSC, BCR Supplement, Virtual Private Networks and the Internet,, April 1996.
[20]Rigdon, J. (March 13,1996). Internet's #1 use: information bureau. *Wall Street Journal*, B5.
[21]Scopus Technology. (1995). Scopus WebTeam Brochure, [Online]. Available FTP: scopus.com.
[22]Rowe, C. (April, 1996,). *Playboy*, 16.
[23]Jenkins, H. (Jan. 30, 1996). Waiting for the web to mature. *Wall Street Journal*, A15.
[24]Rigdon, J. (1995). Forrester Research, *Wall Street Journal*, R20.
[25]Sandberg, J. (March 1,1996). AT&T is facing delays on its plan for internet access. *Wall Street Journal*, A3.
[26]Gilder, G. (Feb. 26, 1996). Telecosm, Goliath at Bay. *Forbes ASAP*, 101.
[27]Birman, K. & Van Renesse, R. (May, 1996). Software for reliable networks. *Scientific American*, 64.
[28](March, 1996,). *Communications News*, 41.
[29]Burstein, D. (1995). *Road Warriors*. New York, NY. Dutton-Penguin, 200.
[30]Dawson, K. (March, 1996,). Computer Telephony Show Daily, 12.
[31]Weber, T. (March 19,1996). MCI matches AT&T's internet offer. *Wall Street Journal*, A3.
[32]Woo, F. (May 6.1996). CTI adds another dimension. Rivka Tadjer CMP Publications, 41.

THE BROAD BAND OF TOMORROW

In this world of information overload, the benumbed citizen no
longer reads or thinks, he watches and feels.
– William Irwin Thompson

T he 20th century was yesterday. Today, image and message have
supplanted text and meaning, the root of reading, and the literary
culture. Fundamentally, America has become a post-literate society that
devalues the ability to comprehend the complexities of the written word
and believes that everything of importance can be converted into and
conveyed as an image.[1] In Japan for example, cable television reaches
only 2.3 percent of homes, compared to nearly 70 percent in the United
States. Forty percent of the United States still receives "free" over-the-air
television.[2]

Now a culture of the magnified message, we live with 30-second
sound bits and jump-cut video editing. True content is being lost in the
search for brevity. We are irretrievably a culture that has bred a class of
individuals who demand the quality and experience that television
provides. For the systems being installed today to fail to deliver the
quality of experience that the audiences of tomorrow will demand would
be an expensive mistake.[3]

Image, the communication medium of the future, will be delivered
optically over hair-thin strands derived from the most common element
of earth's fabric: sand. In March 1996, several R&D labs demonstrated

that they could pump one trillion bits of data per second over a single optical fiber; that is enough to carry 12 million simultaneous conversations or download 100 two-hour movies in one second.

The next generation of architecture for voice, data, and video is, without a doubt, optical fiber. In 50 years, we will communicate from any device, through any medium, using any database. And though optical fiber systems are available for those willing to pay, fiber to the curb is still several years away and fiber to the farm, even further.

Every major communication company has sketched out repeatedly bold plans to extend advanced digital networks to consumers and then retreated when they found out they could not do so cost-effectively, let alone profitably. The good news is that the cost for fiber-optic driven networks and optical-electronics is dropping quickly.

The Device of the Future

As for call centers in the year 2000, estimates project that 25 percent of customer contacts will occur through nonvoice media and 35 percent of service requests will be handled electronically. The percentage of revenue spent on non-face-to-face customer contact is expected to increase from 0.5 percent in 1994 to 3 percent by the year 2002.[4]

The paradigm shift ahead promises elimination of the mainframe orientation, reduction of the dependency on "conversational paradigm," and a full multimedia approach. When the device(s) of the future become defined securely, we know how our customers will call and communicate with us.

Development of these devices will come with the power of the incredible shrinking microchip. Today no one would consider using a $150 Pentium in a light bulb to help it conserve power, but the same Pentium in five years will cost $10, and five years after that, about 10 cents. Conversely, the $500 microprocessor of 10 years from now will possess the power of today's Cray supercomputer plus the power to provide voice processing, interactive voice response, continuous natural speech recognition, and full motion, television-quality interactive video.

Microsoft thinks that this appliance will be the PC transformed into a home device that runs Windows 95 on TVs. Giving PCs the style and convenience of stereo gear, which can be upgraded by simply plugging components together, is a guiding principle.

Even in the United States, where the PC can claim to have permanently etched a place in our cultural psyche, only 35 percent to 40 percent of homes have one. Microsoft envisions a device that would boot up in three to five seconds and would fit on a shelf with other electronic components, playing the audio through an external speaker system or displaying video or graphics that have been pushed through the coming generation of high-definition video disc players. This device would also serve as a telephone or video phone system.

As pervasive as the PC is in its current form, we can pretty safely say that it will not be the device we use for communication. Experts estimate that the PC cannot achieve more than 50 percent market penetration – not enough to establish the Internet as the medium for the masses. The PC is, and will remain for some time, too complicated, too costly, and too unreliable. PC owners have nothing else that fails more frequently than their computers and software. The PC will not be the device you will have to plan for in your call centers, although it will certainly own a share of customer contact methods.

One plausible device just now emerging is the "smart phone." Nokia has released the first generation of smart phones, a combination of mobile telephone, palm-top computer, and personal organizer. The smart phone is possibly the precursor of the next generation of personal-communications devices, new products in wireless communications. The initial steep price, more than $2,000, and the airtime cost incurred in using the device will likely restrict the product's appeal to a narrow, well-heeled clientele.

The Nokia 9000 communicator can download graphics from the Internet and print the data when used, TV remote style, to activate a printer.

Nokia officials expect these smart phones will exhibit a trend similar to that when cellular phones first came out: a fast-growing market will drive prices down quickly.[5] For now, however, the device will work only with European and Asian digital networks.

Similar to the Nokia smart phone, but probably more pragmatic, is a device being developed by Northern Telecom and using Sun Microsystem's interactive network technology to enable its next genera- tion of telephone handsets to access the Internet. Sun's Java software and microprocessors will be incorporated into a new class of inexpensive Internet appliance phones. Northern Telecom is the first company to do this as well as to license the Java chips. These phones can download information onto a small screen with an application that could, at any point, connect the user with a live conversation.

As rapidly as the prototypes are being developed, tested, and proved, it is still too early to forecast what device we will use to communicate in the next ten years. We can say that more than likely the simple telephone will continue to be a dominant fixture in the architecture of contact technology.

Multimedia to the palm top, video on demand to the home, Web browsing without ridiculous delays, video mail, and two-way interactive video are all applications requiring a completely new generation of equipment capable of consuming mega-quantities of information very rapidly. For many experts, Asynchronous Transfer Mode represents the way to communicate between these devices of the future and the companies we want to talk to.

Asynchronous Transfer Mode

If the computer people would ever get together with the telecommuni- cations people and design the perfect networking system, their design would look exactly like Asynchronous Transfer Mode. The widespread acknowledgment of Asynchronous Transfer Mode as the integrating network platform of the future is incredible. Asynchronous Transfer Mode is emerging quickly as the standard for multimedia transmission. Surprisingly, the Internet is among its more prominent consumers. To many, Asynchronous Transfer Mode is not a question of "if" but of "when and where."

Asynchronous Transfer Mode falls within the domain of switching, which is why technologists responsible for their technologies of customer contact should maintain a minimal level of attention and interest in ATM. Asynchronous Transfer Mode is a multi-dimensionally layered suite of protocols, designed to accommodate many media-traffic types from not only other call centers but from the public switched network as well.

ATM is the networking technology anticipated to support full-motion video-type communication devices and appliances in the next few years.

Asynchronous Transfer Mode transmits voice, data, images, and video in 54-byte long "packets," stuffing data packets into streaming spaces between any voice and the video packets. The fixed-cell size enables networks to prioritize voice, delivering a deterministic, predictable response. This is essential when transporting the latency-sensitive communications found particularly in call centers, such as voice and video or other mission-critical interactive-application traffic. For latency-sensitive communications such as voice and video, Asynchronous Transfer Mode devices can be configured to garner specific service quality levels and even be completely nonblocking for all types of media.

This cell-based switching and multiplexing technology appeals because it can send a large volume of multimedia information at high speeds. Asynchronous Transfer Mode delivers a shorter and more deterministic path, meaning faster information flow and more stable performance. With this switching, time drops from many milliseconds (detectable to the human ear) to a few microseconds – virtually real time.

Asynchronous Transfer Mode satisfies the need for an "end-to-end" solution across public, private, or hybrid networks. This technology eliminates the complexity associated with enterprise networking by efficiently consolidating video, voice, and data onto one common network. This concept of a single backbone would help companies organize and consolidate their network infrastructures and monitor their call centers.

Asynchronous Transfer Mode provides scaleable bandwidth at higher speeds than topologies like Fast Ethernet, Fiber Distributed Data Interface (FDDI), or even Copper Distributed Data Interface (CDDI). Vendors from many camps have joined forces, especially those with traditional interests in data, voice, video, and other multimedia networking to develop a common signaling system that can be used across the network, from stem to stern.

The ideal Asynchronous Transfer Mode switch will support the following services, protocols, and interfaces:

- LAN interconnection protocols such as token ring, Ethernet, and FDDI
- IBM protocols: Systems Network Architecture (SNA) services, logical unit switching, and bisynchronous switching
- Frame relay services: fully compliant with user-to-network interface (UNI) and network-to-network interface (NNI) standards.

As such a relatively new and advanced technology, Asynchronous Transfer Mode does not integrate very well with legacy network systems such as LANs, WANs, and other transport mechanisms. In response to these legitimate points, a new generation of products, called intelligent Asynchronous Transfer Mode access products, is in the works. Asynchronous Transfer Mode multiplexes, also called concentrators or aggregators, should jump the legacy hurdle and completely integrate legacy traffic from multiple data, video, and voice networks and convert these data streams into Asynchronous Transfer Mode format for seamless, cost-effective, standards-based transport over wide areas.

New generations of Asynchronous Transfer Mode devices will provide the means to get legacy traffic onto the wide area network. They will have faster processing capabilities plus more ports and cards than their general-purpose predecessors. They focus on switching, and leave access to the stand-alone devices.

Asynchronous Transfer Mode across the wide distance of geographically dispersed call centers requires a serious dollar investment. Currently, access is extremely limited. A serious and underdiscussed issue is that with so much invested in conventional switches, phone companies are likely to keep voice calls on current devices for a long time.

A word of caution: don't underestimate the complexity of Asynchronous Transfer Mode. In spite of prognosticators who exclaim that ATM is technically simple (they, too, get the same glazed over look that Internet proponents get when talking about their technology), it is much more than hacking data into 48-byte pieces, sticking on a 5-byte header, and shipping to some other location in the network.

A pragmatic word of caution for call center technologists: defend your turf when it comes to Asynchronous Transfer Mode. As with every other transport and networking technology, ensure that your combined communications systems give priority to voice traffic; otherwise conversations could be interrupted by traffic from other applications.

Asynchronous Transfer Mode can become the ultimate transport mechanism, providing dynamic bandwidth allocation, end-to-end prioritization, and quality of service guarantees for different types of traffic, such as voice, video, LAN, and System Network Architecture, running over one large distributed network and truly supporting communication from any device, through any medium, and using any database.

Eventually, the power of the microchip and the pipeline to the consumers will be such that Asynchronous Transfer Mode (or at least its speeds) to the desktop will be as common as a telephone line is today. This technology is definitely changing the economics of the Internet. Asynchronous Transfer Mode will make the Internet better suited to the advanced Web sites being contemplated and even to video applications. In recent studies, technology-literate respondents cite Asynchronous Transfer Mode as the basis for future technology.

The line between local and wide area networking becomes increasingly blurred with advances in technology, changes in the telecommunications regulatory environment, and the increased focus of organizations on their primary business endeavors. Call centers will have to be able to support all types of media traffic while maintaining quality of service levels. Cellular communications is one type that will grow quickly as a principal contact method between call center and stakeholder.

Cellular

In 1983, AT&T predicted 900,000 wireless phones would be in use by the year 2000. Today, the United States has some 36 million wireless subscribers, and one is being added every three seconds. In the middle of 1996, each day found 28,000 new cellular subscribers being activated – an average of three new customers per second. Amazingly, although potential for plenty of growth still remains, 85 percent of the population still does not have a cellular phone, and conservative analysts expect 70 million wireless subscribers by the year 2000.[6] In other words, 70 million new possible access points to your company by your stakeholders.

Cellular phone service, which generated $19 billion in revenues last year, is among the fastest growing industries in the country, but the rate of subscriber growth is starting to slow. Market research proves that the technology has expanded out of its original mobile professional market niche to become a widespread consumer service.

The success of cellular phone is somewhat analogous to the McDonald's hamburger phenomena. The great social insight of the McDonald brothers was not that Americans had a particularly enormous appetite for hamburgers but that new highways and new cars created mobility and that workers were commuting long distances and needed a quick meal along the way.[7]

More and more, cellular companies are turning to their call centers as a tool to influence the satisfaction of their subscribers. Long stigmatized by poor customer service and a lack of competition, personal communication services (PCS) are driving cellular companies to advertise heavily and develop intimate customer-retention strategies.

Cellular problems are significant. They include confusing billing, terrible service, free phones that turn out not to be not so cheap because of long-term contracts, and the inability to roam seamlessly from region to region as promised.

An important step in addressing the cellular subscribers' cost concerns is the dual-mode technology that enables a cellular telephone to act as a cordless phone when in range of a home base station. Currently, phones cannot move from one environment to another in mid-call. A wire-line call will simply drop when the caller moves too far away from the base station, just as if a cordless phone were taken too far from its base. The next generation of equipment will address this problem by supporting automatic hand-off to the cellular network in mid-call.

"First bill sticker shock," the cancellation of contracts after customers receive their first and usually much higher than expected bill, is a major problem. Using a proactive customer service out-dialing campaign to customers who were about to receive their first bill, a northeast cellular company started calling new subscribers before they received their first bill to discuss what the customer could expect. This proactive campaign increased significantly the customer retention rate.

The competitive pressures emerging from the advent of PCS have forced cellular services to take the lead in understanding customer dialogue. Most important to the call center technologist will be the effect of this fast-growing source of calls. Hands-free dialing and other wireless phone innovations will drive an increasing numbers of calls coming from these devices. The most significant effect will be the availability of toll-free, 800-number, cellular calls.

For years the American public has been taught that 800 numbers are toll-free calls. But with cellular, they are not. Once an 800 call is passed onto the wire-line long-distance carrier, the 800 customer pays the long-distance charges for the call, but the cellular caller must pay charges for the airtime. Companies should anticipate an influx of calls (and 800-number expense) from cellular callers when toll-free 800 (as well as flat rate) calling becomes available in 1997.

Wireless

Estimates suggest that by 1998, cellular and PCS (personal communication services) wireless users will total 88.3 million devices, with cellular accounting for 37.5 percent, paging, for 41.5 percent, and new personal communications services, 9.7 percent of market share.[8] The PCS market is poised to make the most sweeping impact on the way we take calls from stakeholders.

Personal communication services are newly (re)assigned frequency allocations in response to bandwidth demands and new digital communications technology. This digital-based communications technology (unlike cellular, which is largely analog) provides greater capacity and security against eavesdropping as well as a way to transmit both voice and data combined (but not necessarily better voice quality). The three types of PCS are unlicensed PCS for wireless LANs and PBXs, narrow-band PCS (900mHz) for two-way paging, and broadband PCS (1.8 GHz) for wide area (microcell) cellular-type communications.

Early tests by Sprint Wireless in the Washington, D.C. area have shown that with the quality of the PCS services and a lower pricing structure than cellular, customers are using their PCS phones in much the same way they use regular telephones. The PCS Network in Washington, D.C. has gained more than 60,000 customers since its November 1995 launch, expecting to reach the 60,000 subscriber mark only by the end of 1996, putting it 10 months ahead of schedule – and occasionally overwhelming the network's customer billing and order processing systems.[9]

Unlike cellular, which experiences peak traffic during morning and late afternoon drive times, the PCS technology has a nearly even flow of calls throughout the day. Interestingly, Sprint's PCS also receives as many calls from the wire-line networks as it sends to them. This is a sharp contrast to the rest of the wireless industry, where as much as 80 percent of the traffic crossing network boundaries is estimated to be going from portable phones to regular telephones.

Voice communications are not the only ones that are being delivered over wireless networks. The use of wireless modems is increasing dramatically. AT&T is beginning to provide cellular-based modem services and is installing modem pools in 12 of its top cellular markets. The company plans to have modem pools covering 90 percent of its cellular market nationwide by July 1997. I may not call your call center on my car phone now; I may just dial in from my wireless laptop.

In addition to cellular and PCS, other wireless communications technologies are on the horizon. Motorola has announced recently a two-way digital radio designed to compete with advanced cellular telephones. These new types of devices provide voice communications, fax receipt, and paging. These new devices are expected to be cheaper and operate more efficiently than standard cellular phones.

Wireless can have several connotations. For the purposes of this book, a distinction must be made between wireless used outside of buildings and the wireless systems emerging inside of call centers. Both will have a dramatic impact on the technology of customer contact. The more wireless phones (and modems) out there, the more calls enterprises will receive. Wireless inside of call centers will have a significant effect as well because as the reliability of the technology advances, agents and employees will become ever more mobile.

Mobility in call centers, the untethering of agents from their stations, has released a change in perspective by call center management as to the true extent that their employees have "been talking in circles," that circle being the three or four foot length of their handset or headset cord.

Within 10 years, wireless telephones and similar devices will be as common in our pockets, on our wrists, and on our waists as telephones are in our homes. Voice traffic to call centers will increase in relation to this device explosion. The effect on each company can be determined only by understanding the nature of your stakeholder population.

Video

Video is the most natural of the data types and is in line with the trend of providing more complex and sophisticated transactions. I have never met professional basketball player Hakeem Olajuwon, but thanks to TV, I feel as if I have known him all of my life. Video penetrates the human psyche, and its use of parallel channels of communications (gesture, gaze, and speech) is the essence of human communication.

Face-to-face contact is crucial to sophisticated product sales. Many industries consider face-to-face contact the key for sales. Through video calls, the expertise can be located separately from the point-of-sale. Experts can be used more efficiently and effectively, and the customer has access to better service with greater convenience. Video is an innovative way for companies to distinguish themselves and remain competitive in a rapidly changing business environment.

One study by Mentis Corporation indicated that 76 percent of banking service customers felt that visual contact was essential for financial product sales. Overall, 62 percent (and 72 percent of automatic teller machine users) indicated a willingness to shop for financial products via interactive video.[10] Wherever there are multiple people who may receive person-to-person video connections, there is an application for a video call center application.

Video provides a "high-touch" addition that enhances customer service dramatically. Being able to see the person on the other end of the line, show the problem directly, and exchange information, image, and data along with voice is the very next best thing to being physically with the customer on demand. This increases customer satisfaction and trust, and enables more complex and sophisticated transactions.

These advantages of live contact are well understood for voice calls. To date, these advantages have been overlooked for video because most of the industry is concentrating on point-to-point connections and multimedia, and forgetting that a call center exists at the other end of the line.

Video calls are expected to originate initially from video kiosks. With a kiosk, the caller is at a known location, such as a video touch screen display in a storefront. New video-based applications provide multimedia and compressed video in real time via ISDN to off-site video-based locations such as a kiosk or an automatic teller machine. Since ISDN is currently the most pervasive method for carrying video calls, kiosks and other callers can be located anywhere that ISDN reaches. Once the video signal reaches the inside of your call center, different technology issues begin to emerge.

Most technologists see video coming, and they know that if they are not dabbling in it they will get left behind. What they are doing is very limited and on a pilot project basis, with two or three agents dedicated to a video or Internet but very much separated from the full call center activity in an effort to understand better the implications for the stakeholder relationship.

Video over LANs has some serious drawbacks, primarily because of the "bursty" nature of data traffic controlled by data gateways. Router prioritization of data traffic often puts data traffic before video (and voice) traffic, which creates latency problems such as picture jerkiness. Also, a limited number of simultaneous video connections can be supported over today's existing topologies (which are still very expensive).

Another problem with video is it has no good quality software; video has only CODECs, which require more powerful central processing units (CPUs) than are present in the general PC population. Completely software-only CODECs are expected by 1998. This is an area where desktop video collaboration is taking the lead.

To understand the future of the interactive video-driven call center, look at the cable companies. Some experts believe that consumers will continue to rebel at anything less than television quality, although no one disputes that video technology is improving quickly. Even today's fastest common modems at 28,800 bps are only fast enough to permit good audio and jerky, compression-blemished (but recognizable) video output at 10 frames per second, compared with television images that flash at a rate of 30 times per second.

For video to work in the call center, the video signal flow stream must have all the features of call routing and reporting that are available to voice calls: skills-based routing, real-time status, and comprehensive management reports. From the old days of call hold, call transfer, call forward, and call conferencing, we will move to video hold, video transfer, video forward, video call waiting, and video conference capabilities – much more difficult to provide than even most emerging platforms can support.

But today, traffic and activity are very low, and the cost to integrate video throughout the center is ridiculously high. Video is not an easy technology to integrate with most other technologies. Video call centers constitute one market where early adopters will face major system upgrades somewhere down the road. In its current technical form, video is an unrealistic expectation in call centers because we are a culture weaned on television quality. Until we achieve that interactive quality seen on the Jetsons and Star Trek, video just won't show well. Video will remain limited in scope for a long time because the cost justification is going to be long in coming for most industries.

Speech

Spoken input to computers is just now passing the threshold of practicality. The last decade has witnessed tremendous improvement in speech recognition technology, to the extent that high performance DSPs, codecs, and algorithms are becoming available. Because processor costs have dropped so dramatically, speech processing and CTI are fast becoming a natural combination.

Applied to microprocessors, Moore's Law of Productive Technology has proven that available computing power quadruples every 30 months. Applied to DSPs is a lesser known but equally effective axiom known as Turner's law, postulated by Brough Turner, an executive at Natural MicroSystems and a founder of the Multi Vendor Integration Protocol (MVIP) industry standard. Turner's law is similar to Moore's law, although specific to DSP microprocessors.

Turner's Law is applied to the doubling of processing power per chip roughly every 20 months. One measurement of a microprocessor's computing power is measured in Mips, million instructions per second. These measurements are a critical factor in the use of DSPs and in the boards used for telecommunication applications. Turner's law can be applied equally to the growth of Mips per dollar or Mips per cubic area of space.

Previous generations of telecommunications and DSP-based technologies were physically unable to keep pace with this axiom of Turner's law. The hardware of the technology itself impeded the development of applications, and the implementation of the raw processing power is becoming readily available every 20 months or so.

These systems can use voice recognition, flexible vocabulary recognition, word spotting, natural language recognition, and text to speech, among others, to determine meaning and search for answers to customer-spoken inquiries. Another important technical factor is whether your caller needs continuous speech recognition or can respond in short, one-word blurbs. Continuous speech recognition systems let the caller talk at a near normal pace, whereas a noncontinuous system requires the caller to pause in between every word. Which would you expect to become the preferred and more widely accepted method?

Look for speech recognition applications to begin to appear in 411 applications, stock quotes, telephone security (caller identification), and cellular and wireless markets where driving or operating equipment while talking is discouraged.

A fully functional, natural language recognition application is used for 411 information systems in the Philadelphia market and for a few long-distance dialing companies. Otherwise, only a few reliable working commercial examples of speech recognition applications are front ending call centers.

Should video not become available, customer-telephone interfaces could conceivably become fully automated verbal inquiries and transactions. I anticipate, however, that the technology will be here long before our culture is willing to use it. For the moment, talk may be cheap, but speech recognition is still very expensive.

Speech recognition is definitely one of the sexiest technologies, influenced by the animated conversations of HAL in 2001 (that television thing again), but the prices still and will continue to scare most customers away. Like video, speech recognition will become useful and functional when we achieve movie quality. When it happens, look for profound influence on the markets we communicate with, because once we can do recognition, we can then do language translation, and this opens a whole world of interaction with stakeholders from anywhere around the globe.

The Interactive Cable Modem

By the year 2000, Forrester Research predicts as many as 7 million homes may have cable modems. Seven million by 2000? That is only a small percent of the U.S. population considering that almost 70 percent of the country has cable TV. Depending on how you look at it, the cup could be really empty or not very full at all.

Cable is creeping up on us all as a medium that can handle television-quality broadband services to the home. With cable companies reaching nearly 66 percent of the country, they can, with the right equipment, deliver far more services than the telephone companies' twisted pair copper wire that links most phones. The cable companies are working on high-speed modems that will link and work with both the PC and the TV – modems that will interact at as much as 1,000 times the speed of conventional modems. These new modems will allow customers to suck in data from the Internet at speeds almost 100 times faster than ISDN.

Cable companies are combining high-capacity fiber-optic lines with coaxial cables into the home, so that they can deliver voice, video, and data simultaneously. But turning this link into a functioning and consumer-accepted two-way path for consumer communications services is a difficult process that no cable company has yet pulled off.

Some analysts are already predicting that cable modems will supplant ISDN basic-rate interface service, which, while also growing, has yet to retain a significant foothold. Even cable though, as a shared medium, will dwindle to ISDN rates as the number of customers on the systems rises (at least according to Bill Gates).

A critical challenge for the cable industry is to deploy more fiber distribution and reduce the number of customers sharing the cable bandwidth. Many problems must still be worked out, including power requirements and security mechanisms to prevent snooping.

Can cable companies support voice and data customers? Voice and data services differ from each other markedly – voice and data only remotely resemble blowing HBO and Showtime into the back of someone's television set.

Cable TV operators may be the least equipped to provide the full-motion interactivity demanded of the broadband future because they do not have the capital or the technology. They are entering the race loaded with the debt of wiring 60 percent of the country with coaxial cable, low profitability, and a lingering reputation for poor service. In short, the cable companies have to learn a new business – telephony.[11] Would you want to rely on your cable company to dial 911 when your child is choking?

The promise of cable was that you could interact with the network, ordering a nearly endless supply of movies or shopping from home. However, the real motivation of the cable companies is not to deliver "Snow White and the Seven Dwarfs" on demand but to deliver a phone call to your mother. The ulterior motive of the cable people is that they want a slice of the $300 billion dollar phone service and carrier market. Paul Kagen Associates' analyst Sharon Armbrust estimates that by 2005, cable companies will generate $5.9 billion in telephone revenues. By then, the market for phone service is expected to double to nearly $300 billion.

Even the leaders of the cable industry admit that they have yet to understand when interactive TV will become a reality. "We are still not sure when true interactive TV will come," admits James Robbins, CEO of Cox Communications Inc.[12]

Wireless cable allows customers to download Internet-based information almost seven times faster than do most phone-based systems. Wireless cable uses small rooftop antennae that must be positioned for a direct line of sight to a customer's home. Dense cities are particularly difficult. Wireless phones are prone to glitches and also tie up a phone line (that is how the data part of the transaction is sent).

Cable modems are definitely on the horizon, but I would not be too concerned about their impact on communication. After all, they are not out to drive video two-way interaction; they want your customers' telephone service. This, like the growth of cellular and PCS, simply reinforces the telephone as the device of communication preference for much longer than other visionaries would expect.

Other Broadband Backbones

Other technologies viewed from the stakeholder connection perspective include satellite connections and digital subscriber line services from the telephone companies. Satellites offer a unique promise because no other technology, including television, has grown more quickly. They are important because when satellite-based products become available with two-way interactive capabilities, the entire country becomes available for access. Fiber to the farm becomes a nonissue as you can interact from anywhere that would traditionally not have sophisticated services. Coupled with the general population migration away from cities and into rural areas, satellites with their dish-shaped antenna on rooftops have intriguing possibilities as another method of stakeholder connection.

Unlike high-orbiting satellite systems of the past, Low Earth Orbiting Satellites (LEOS) from Motorola, AT&T, General Electric, and Lockheed Martin will provide reduced transmission times (satellite phone connections today are plagued with an annoying quarter-second delay) and power consumption. Serious systems on the drawing board include Motorola's Iridium (66 satellites for $3.4 billion) and Teledesic (Bill Gates and Craig McCaw, 840 satellites for $9 billion).

Satellites are still notoriously fickle as far as reliability is concerned. The Chinese have difficulty even getting them to launch without blowing up. Recently, an electrical fault wiped out more than 50 percent of the capacity of a $300 million communications satellite delivering services to Canada, temporarily disrupting television service and data transmission.

Satellites will probably be slow with regard to data speeds, and the services will be very expensive. Two-way interactive satellite-based services will provide cost-justified access in remote areas. But how many of your stakeholders live in these areas? Wholesale consumer-based satellite services are at least 15 years off.

High-bit-rate Digital Subscriber Line (HDSL) technology and its cousin ADSL (Asymmetrical Digital Subscriber Loop) represent a promising technology being developed by the Bell companies that will offer repeaterless spans of 12,000 feet over existing telephone lines. The ADSL technology sends megabits of data over ordinary twisted pair lines by using frequencies as high as 1 million cycles per second.

Much attention is being focused on ADSL for home multimedia delivery. This technology provides transmission at 6 megabits per second from the phone company central office to your desktop and up to 640 Kps for transmission going the other way. This unbalanced channel configuration fits many data networking patterns, where small requests for data, such as database queries and Internet requests, are met with large amounts of data to send back to the customer.

Asymmetrical Digital Subscriber Loop technology is promising but does have a couple of obstacles, including a lack of standards (even more so than the CTI industry) and physical limitations in-bred into the local telephone networks. This technology can only work out from a Central

Office at a maximum distance of 18,000 feet. Sensitive and expensive signal detection chips are required because signals at these 1 million cycles per second frequencies over copper wire lose power in a relatively short distance. Also, PC-based ADSL interface cards have yet to be built or, at least, proved to be efficient and reliable.[13] Several unproven ADSL devices out there include regular ADSL modems, modems with routing functions, and PCs with ADSL capabilities.

In mid-1996, ADSL services of 1.5 megabytes per second were tested, followed with a 6 megabyte per second trial with 150 users at a commercial user site, proving the viability of the trials for Internet access and remote workers. For the next several years, expect varied services and flexible pricing schemes.

The technology is far from being standard or having the common interfaces that can sustain large volumes. The reason ADSL and satellites are important to the managers of contact technology is that these are two, of several, different paths that callers will take as they communicate with enterprises. As with the Internet, the number of your stakeholders actually communicating with these technologies may never be substantial, but you should pay attention to the influence they will have.

Conclusion

The future will inevitably bring cheap, reliable technology that allows customers, stakeholders, and agents to establish live, full-motion television-quality audio and video connections for applications like teleconferencing and videoconferencing.

The key to an enterprise's success now depends mainly on its ability to quickly and smoothly introduce new technology into its network and to consolidate multiple types of traffic onto a single, high-performance multimedia network. Today's organizations, faced with escalating demands for higher bandwidth as the cost of maintaining separate networks increases, are seeking cost-effective solutions to consolidate data, voice, and video.

To reach the call center nirvana of fully interchangeable voice, text, and video will require a standard compressed data format in which users can create and send messages without worrying about what kind of device is on the other end. We are a long way from this.

In the past, a call center was music on hold. Now, a call center is intelligent queuing, skills-based routing, and menu in queue.

The broadband call center of the future will need a system for managing multiple priorities – a traffic management capability that allows different types of data traffic to be segregated, prioritized, and managed according to application demands. Agents can be distributed anywhere, and traditional ACD feature sets can be applied to any type of call, i.e., skills-based routing, real-time status, and comprehensive management reporting.

The future is immense and no one person can stay on top of these developing technologies. The only sure safe investment is with vendors who are at least dabbling in, but not promoting, these technologies. Asynchronous Transfer Mode is a certain bet, and I wouldn't hesitate at all to build a migration plan toward it.

The comfort level you should have with your call center technology can probably be determined by the depth and extent to which a vendor can answer a few future-oriented questions.

Ask your vendor about its

- migration path to open, standards-based products;
- track record in investment protection;
- experience in CTI;
- partnerships with other information technology industry leaders; and
- planned migration path to Asynchronous Transfer Mode.

Broadband for the masses? No way, says Bill Gates, not for another 20 years. For certain we are a long way from an economy and enterprise technology base where an agent or worker will be able to do all things from all desks. The technology is assuredly close to being here, but the costs and the culture are not. No matter how user friendly the broadband technologies and networks of tomorrow may be, they will all likely require some degree of thought and skill to access deeply and meaningfully. Between the narrow-band of today and the unlimited bandwidth of tomorrow lies the pragmatic middle band.

---

[1]Kaplan, M. (May 7,1995). Illiteracy a looming crisis in the information age. *San Francsico Examiner*, C5

[2]Rather, D. (March 20,1996). Eye on America, televison news segment. CBS News.

[3]McQuillan, J. (March, 1996). No bits like show bits. BCR, 80.

[4](1996, March 12). Gartner Group, CTI Expo.

[5](March 15, 1996,). *Wall Street Journal*, B2.

[6]Naik, G. (March 26, 1996,). Cellular show offers broad spectrum. *Wall Street Journal*, B6.

[7]Halberstam, D. (1993). *The Fifties*. New York, NY, Villard Books.

[8]Mathias, C. (Feb. 12, 1996). Farpoint Group: slide presentation. PBX96 Conference, Washington, DC.

[9](April 4, 1996). CITA special report. Wireless 96 annual convention, wire report.

[10](1996). Teloquent brochure. Teloquent Communications, Billerica, MA.

[11]Finneran, M. (March, 1996,). Cable modems madness. BCR, 70.

[12]Grtover, R. (April 8, 1996). Special report: The Coming Telescramble. Business Week, 75.

[13]SW Bell Initiates ADSL" Communications Week, May 27, 1996 www.commweek.com.

THE MIDDLE BAND GAP IN BETWEEN

Good things may come to those who wait, but only those things that are left over from those who hustle.
– Abe Lincoln (supposedly)

The new economy, the new enterprise, the new work force, and the new technology are linked inextricably. They enable and drive one another. If you can understand how the new technology corresponds to the new internetworked enterprise, you can begin to forge a strategy for competing in the new economy.[1] The new economy will incorporate markets that were essentially closed prior to a convergence of all of these trends and technologies.

Nowhere is this convergence more dramatic than between the telephone and the computer. Every telecommunications vendor feels the competitive heat from a computer industry that not only is now open to telephony but wants to provide it. Confidently buoyed by the increasing processing power of the chip, the computer world is dashing boldly into competitive warfare, with the PC and the server as their foot soldiers.

The battle plan is simple: surround with peripherals and conquer. First these PCs did reporting; then, voice mail; now, CTI; and eventually, the switching itself. Like a swarming army of ants, their pursuit of telephony is unmerciful and relentless; their battlefield is the middle band of the next two to five years. Very few, if any, of the PC generals are even looking at the broadband future, which is just too far away right now.

As engaging and absorbing as a discussion about the broad band of tomorrow can be, its pragmatic analysis does little to satisfy the immediate need to plan for tomorrow, next week, or next year. Because so much of the broad band has yet to be defined, the middle-band, if understood, can take the "in" out of "indecisive."

In this book, "middle band" is defined as a window of time existing for the two to five years of the close of this millennium and consists of certain types of technologies currently under development. To Microsoft's Bill Gates, for example, cable modems are mere middle band.

In the battle for the middle ground, all sides share a common vision of victory. The client/server people, ACD/PBX, stand-alone ACD, NetWare, Asynchronous Transfer Mode, and most other communication technologies have the same end result in mind.

Their vision pertains to managing the electronic gap between you and your customers (i.e., telephone, e-mail, Internet, fax, wireless PDAs, or TV) and creating an opportunity to establish a dialogue. No one disputes that, in today's business environment, improving your relationships with your customers is your best competitive advantage. When customers contact you, they have little patience for long interactions or future follow-ups. They want their needs – whether to buy, how to deal with debt, or deal with a service problem – met quickly and efficiently.

The Immediate Speed of Information

Little notice was made when overnight delivery services supplanted postal mail 15 years ago. Consumers used to have to write away for things in catalogs, but now they pick up the phones and dial an 800 number on impulse. As inferior a device as the fax machine may be, China's Tiananmen Square revolution was the first fomented by fax because of the Chinese government's inability to censor or slow the immediacy of dissidents' fax communications (mostly to the west coast of the United States).

In an economy based on bits, the immediacy of information becomes a key driver and an essential variable in economic activity and business success.[2] Consumers and businesses alike are finding this to be the case.

Your company may spend millions on sales, marketing, and advertising, but if you are not prepared to handle immediately the calls your campaign generates, your efforts are stunted at best. To use call center technology to really improve customer service requires retooling, not re-engineering, for all concerned. Rethinking the true phone-centricness of your company will create opportunities to lower costs and increase benefits.

Using the new tools of re-engineering, we leave behind the era characterized by customers as providers of information ("What is your shoe size?"). Now, customers are consumers of information ("What sizes do you have?"). Information immediacy is the new ammunition of technologists. And digital networks of thin copper and optical highways are the backbones supporting the reality of immediate information.

The infrastructure of the enterprise provides the backbone for the new enterprise. This infrastructure enables an organization to move beyond the old hierarchy because layers of management are not required when instant information is available electronically. The infrastructure enables the enterprise to function cohesively by providing corporate information for decision making and new competitive enterprise applications that transcend autonomous business units or teams. The enterprising computing sector – communications networks for businesses such as ACDs, PBXs, media server interfaces, object management and exchange, standardized statistics collection, storage and databases to circulate information through these networks, and groupware to help employees use that information collaboratively – is experiencing rapid growth as rigid corporate hierarchies flatten into decentralized work teams.

Indisputably at the core of this vision of customer centricity is the call center, with its technology of customer contact. Call centers can no longer be considered islands unto themselves. They cut across all departments, affecting everything, everywhere. Those call centers that did operate as islands are now interconnected to sophisticated networks and huge databases.

The integration of most company call centers into the strategic technology planning of most companies has a single identifiable point where the importance of that technology of customer contact moves from being tactical to strategic. This transition occurs at different paces for different companies but often can be identified as the point where senior executives suddenly become interested in the value of their stakeholder-contact technology.

The Tactical vs. the Strategic

The tactical employment of technology is made with a limited or immediate end in view. Often tactical deployment of technology serves the short term and is reactive. For the most part, the very nature of call centers and the technology they use has always been tactical, with little planning for long-term proactive consequences.

On the computer side, the incredible exponential growth in the power of the chip makes impossible planning on anything in the immediate two to five years. For the most part, the only long-term, strategic planning has come from the data world, not because they are particularly good at it but because that's all they could do. In the world of PCs and client/server, we cannot tell where the technology will be in two years; five years is easier.

Strategic planning involves the long-term, big picture. How many call center managers huddle in executive conferences with the CEO and his team to discuss the call center's role in five years? Until fairly recently, none that I knew of.

The following chart compares several tactical functions of the traditional call center with the equivalent function in the strategic call center orientation. The graphic also depicts the migration from the narrow-band limitation of today to the broadband expectations of the future. In between lies the middle band of now.

The Tactical	The Strategic
Cost center	Revenue focus
Reactive	Proactive
Volume orientation	Service orientation
Entry-level personnel	Professional personnel
Telecom & CC managers	CEOs, EVP & CIOs
Uniform, anonymous	Personalized, homogenous
Broad-scale campaigns	Targeted campaigns
Large, Centralized centers	Decentralized, Departmental centers
POTS	PANS
Infrastructure	Infostructure
PBX-based ACD	Client/server ACD
LAN	WAN
Internet	IntraNet
Computer telephone	Multimedia
Wired switch	Wireless
Hardware centric	Software centric
Call control	Mixed-media control
Not real time	Near real time

(Left margin: NARROW BAND • Middle divider: MIDDLE BAND • Right margin: BROAD BAND)

Technology Sources Add to Confusion

One reason the computer industry intimidates the entire telecommunications industry, not just the call centers, is the overwhelming number and sources for technology-based solutions. The list of technology providers includes the following:

- switch manufacturers
- computer manufacturers
- application software providers
- CTI-application providers
- voice-processing manufacturers
- system integrators
- service bureaus
- consultants and predictive dialers.

The technology sources are often confusing to sort out; furthermore, the applications themselves have spawned entire industries of experts and providers. When we inventory the often disparate technologies administered and managed currently in all but the smallest organizations, the list mounts rapidly.

Today's approach requires integrating many pieces. The following list demonstrates the complexities of integrating technologies that can be used in customer collaboration. Software and hardware are available that help an organization track seamlessly and manage every aspect of the interaction between its company and its customers, from complete order and problem histories to prices quoted, defects resolved, and sales cycles closed.

Options for Desktop Productivity:

- Business process automation
- Reporting and statistics applications
- Sales force automation
- Helpdesk automation

Call Processing:

- PBX switching
- Automatic call distribution
- CTI server
- Systems management and reports
- Intelligent queuing
- Directory services
- Predictive dialing
- Fax servers
- Intelligent routing
- Voice mail
- Call blending
- Legacy applications
- Interactive voice response
- Customer databases

Inputs:

- Touch-tone telephone

- Rotary phone
- Internet
- Fax
- Desktop PC
- Client/server PCs
- Voice recognition
- Local processing
- Text-to-speech
- Host database access
- Modems
- Multimedia PC connectivity
- Screen phones

The integration of these systems and architecture is often based on principles defined by business managers rather than by technologists. These technically savvy mangers favor none and look capably at all of these technologies as a strategic, integrated whole. Their concept differs markedly from the stovepipes of the old hierarchies. Models involving the multiplicities of technology must encompass many elements, including the business culture, applications, information, and technology.

The ultimate architecture defines standards for systems within the organization. As this architecture becomes implemented, the enterprise has an infrastructure upon which to become integrated. The best, and so far easiest, emerging platform on which to accomplish this enterprise-wide integration of technology is client/server.

A client/server-based tool for business re-engineering provides informational interaction among all functional areas, using both telephony and computer systems integration to provide maximum customer service, quality, sales effectiveness, and operational efficiency. At the same time, such architectures provide a platform for entrepreneurial innovation in the use of computers by business teams while maintaining an enterprise capability.

Whether your customers contact your enterprise via the phone, fax, e-mail, or WWW, every interaction is stored in the same central database of customer and product information. Interactive voice response (IVR) and voice processing are examples of two middle-band technologies influenced dramatically by client/server technologies.

Voice Processing and IVR

Voice messaging and IVR are fast becoming the second most-used (not necessarily the most-liked) form of communication in the world. The technology of voice processing began in the business world but is now proliferating rapidly in consumer markets.

This proliferation has created a whole new mode of communication – our world has become the world of the magnified message. Trying to call anybody directly these days has become a gigantic waste of time. In the business world alone, 75 percent of all calls go into voice mail. The success of IVR and voice mail revolves very much around understanding that consumer expectations for a phone contact differ from those of a business person.

Frost & Sullivan maintains that IVR and voice-messaging systems will continue to grow, with revenues expected to increase from $1.5 billion in 1996 to more than $3.7 billion by 2002. This represents an average annual growth rate of 18.7 percent.[3]

Interactive voice response increases service levels and decreases operational costs. Furthermore, callers prefer IVR if the application is good. With IVR, human resources are used more effectively and barriers to information transference are removed.

Interactive voice response and voice mail provide a viable, culturally accepted ACD bypass with no holding and no busy signals, and can be anonymous, fast, and accurate. These voice-processing technologies can also handle growth and call-traffic spikes more efficiently; you don't have to add bodies, just ports. Through voice processing and IVR, supporters of client/server architectures are finding the path of least resistance into the call center environments.

Studies have shown that after the initial contact, more than one half of callers accept IVR and voice mail. I am not certain that my grandmother has yet taken to speaking and interacting with a machine, but most of the country is no longer surprised when the pleasant voice of Silicon Sally invariably answers the phone. In every case, the success of any voice-processing application requires an understanding of its users. For example, if your callers are among the 30 percent of Americans who have rotary telephones, IVR may not work.

We shall see an increasing demand for the integration of voice-technology applications. Unified messaging and the universal mailbox will further empower workers and agents at their desktop, particularly in the informal call centers that handle multiple streams of stakeholder input.

New voice-processing technology such as speech recognition, speaker verification, and text-to-speech will be integrated increasingly in telecommunications applications. These emerging technologies will begin to enter the mainstream market by the end of 1996 and will build rapidly over the next several years.

Increased use of speech recognition in IVR applications will improve call handling effectiveness, particularly for the population of callers who are technically intimidated or do not have a PC or even a touch-tone telephone. The bad news, however, is that IVR is hard to program, requires staff expertise, and is in a constant state of obsolescence. Interactive voice response tends to drain resources from the enterprise's core business, and vendor support is often poor. Moreover, implementations and changes often take too long, and true costs are always higher than expected.

If used correctly, IVR can yield a high return on investment. Increased

LAN connectivity for IVR will widen user accessibility.

Inbound/Outbound

Every enterprise has contractions and expansions in call flow. At some times during the business day, employees are contacting stakeholders; at other times, the stakeholders are establishing contact. The worst thing that can happen to a stakeholder-proactive enterprise is when a caller hangs up.

Companies can achieve new levels of customer satisfaction and a competitive advantage by assigning staff to make proactive service calls during periods of low inbound activity. Abandoned call follow-up works best because the agent, if the information is available, can have the customer profile before calling the customer who abandoned the call. Potential applications for integrated inbound and outbound contact processes would be cable companies calling subscribers to confirm new service or restored service after an outage, financial firms welcoming new accounts, utility companies scheduling service calls and meter readings, health-care providers arranging and reminding patients of appointments, catalog companies notifying customers of special promotions, and manufacturers advising customers of product availability.

Successful predictive outbound dialing depends on answer-detect capabilities, which screen out unsuccessful call attempts (such as fax and answering-machine responses) and recognize country-specific telephone protocols to support international calling.

By merging inbound and outbound technology, a company can fully utilize its work force, address rapidly changing priorities, combine inbound and outbound call strategies, and consolidate reporting. Comprehensive inbound and outbound call handling capabilities will prove to provide solutions that dramatically increase the operational efficiencies of the agents and the technology. In call center environments, the activity of contact efforts will be paced largely by the rate of inbound calls. It is the intelligent outbound servers that now integrate self-pacing predictive dialers. Disparate databases can now be used to support and track the complex flow of information on any mix of inbound/outbound projects.

Databases

At the heart of the technologies of customer contact, one or more databases track details on every contact made by employees, agents, and workers. Each database must be integrated seamlessly with other corporate information resources.

The new technologies of data carry a host of new names, including data warehousing, data mining, and on-line analytical processing (OLAP). These tools are intended to help businesses turn data upside down, providing complex views from different business perspectives. They apply to call centers of any size, from formal to remote.

To make pivotal pricing and purchasing decisions, a company wants to know what each department is doing on a day-to-day, even hour-to-hour basis. Traditional call center performance criteria such as average handling time, average speed of answer, and average waiting time can now be extended to include other performance values – for example, how many times a customer's record in the database has been accessed during the month, and from what source.

Enough experience has been gained to prove that a major part of any re-engineering effort is with the data conversion. Tying these often disparate systems together or combining them in usable ways remains challenging. Many large companies still use old style, flat-file mainframe databases; tapping legacy databases has been an incredible source of frustration for many companies.

A new-generation name for an old repository is data warehouse. Data warehouses are often compendiums of data drawn from older, multiple computer systems. The problem facing most companies today is that the data reside usually in such multiple systems as accounting, manufacturing, customer support, inventory and human resources. While these old databases can store reliably a world of bits and bytes, they cannot slice and dice the data.

But data alone are only part of the equation. You may have massive amounts of data, but whether you have massive amounts of information is another question. Converting raw data into market analysis, customer trends, and new revenue and skills-based routing capabilities is proving quickly to be a valuable discipline.

Tapping into the resources of all of their different databases, National Car Rental knows the precise number of automobiles to hold for late booking and how many cars to hold for their high-paying, Pareto customers. Delta Airlines deals with up to 700,000 industry-wide airfare changes every three hours. Technology is applied to capture information on-line and to update information banks in real time, giving an accurate picture or enabling the management of a production process minute by minute.

Consider this example of a major retail company using data as real information. Wal-Mart discovered that people who come into their stores on Thursday to buy Huggies Diapers tend to purchase 19 additional items while they are in the store. Thursday's beer buyers only buy beer. So every Thursday, Huggies are on sale, luring customers to fill their carts and make the cash registers ring. Wal-mart even changes the floor layout to ensure that customers bump into those 19 other popular products.[4]

Such are the ramifications of a fundamental but complex technology – the database. Virtually every business process draws on one, and a smart call center technologist will pay attention, at least peripherally, to this discipline. Database competency will be ultimately a requirement for skills-based routing and managers of customer contact technology will learn the intricacies and requirements of databases.

How Sophisticated Can This Stuff Be, Anyway?

If technology managers in telecommunications are overwhelmed by the elements of the data world, the data people certainly can be dumbfounded by the sophistication of the telephone system. Pervasive cultural thinking among senior business executives tends to underestimate the level of sophistication in technology we use in call centers, businesses, and homes. A tremendously large population of managers were weaned on computers when computers were easy. I still wonder why I had to learn BASIC programming in college.

In the computer business, Microsoft receives about 750,000 customers calls for help every month – that's 9 million callers a year. Symantec's 505-employee Customers Service Center in Eugene, Oregon fields 15,000 calls per day, and IBM answers close to 200,000 calls a day. Third-party support lines field another estimated 100,000 calls per month. Added to this figure has to be the approximately 500,000 calls each month to every other technical support-related call center.[5] This adds up to a considerable amount of time that callers spend on hold, while waiting for "the next available agent to assist you."

Even something as seemingly simple such as accepting a call and then placing it on hold ("Please hold, all agents are busy. Your call will be. . . .") has enormous ramifications in the operating efficiency of processing any call. Big money may be made – saved actually – by calculating precisely the amount of time a caller can expect to be waiting on hold. Telling callers how long they have to wait can be a tremendous service to them; they want to turn on the speakerphone and go get a cup of coffee if the wait will be long.

Call centers are no different. For example, queue holding time is an example of one element of a commonly predicted value in the call center. What is a queue? Queuing is the sequencing of callers in a logical line before the next available agent or application becomes available. Today, we have multiple queues by media type; fax, voice mail, e-mail, and voice. Eventually we will have a single multimedia queue.

Calculating and announcing the estimated hold time in a queue is tricky business. Its mathematical complexities and sophistication should not be underestimated. The following abstract from a patent for an expected waiting time indication arrangement describes a new way to calculate the estimated waiting time of a call. Note the new term, "enqueue."

Abstract

In an automatic call distribution (ACD) system, an improved estimated waiting time arrangement derives a more accurate estimate of how long a call that is or may be enqueued in a particular queue will have to wait before being serviced by an agent, by using the average rate of advance of calls through positions of the particular queue. For a dequeued call, the arrangement determines the call's individual rate of advance from one queue position to the next toward the head of the queue. It then uses this individual rate to recompute a weighted average rate of advance through the queue derived from calls that preceded the last-dequeued call through the queue. To derive a particular call's estimated waiting time, the arrangement multiplies the present weighted average rate of advance by the particular call's position number in the queue. The arrangement may be called upon to update the derivation at any time before or while the call is in queue. Also, the arrangement performs the estimated waiting time derivation separately and individually for each separate queue.

The arrangement advantageously takes into consideration the effect of ACD features that affect the estimated waiting time, including changes in the numbers of agents that are serving the queue due to agent login and logout, multiple split/skill queuing, agents with multiple skills or in multiple splits, priority queuing, interflow, intraflow, and call-abandonment rates.

Ironically, just as the Heisenberg Uncertainty Principle predicts, you can never be able to tell a caller his or her expected waiting time with 100 percent accuracy, but you can get pretty close. No algorithm exists that can factor in an event where, for example, 20 agents are on the phone, 10 people are backed up, and 11 of those agents hang up at the same time.

A common characteristic of any call center, regardless of how it is classified, is the queuing, enqueuing, and dequeuing of calls (and other media as well, such as fax). In the world of constantly changing call center definitions and descriptions, categorizing and classifying them is nearly impossible. Although an infinite number of permutations exist on the call center definition scale, generally four distinct breeds of call centers emerge. Each differs from the others and serves a specific marketing purpose. All four benefit from technical development in the others, although to migrate a feature from one to the other takes time and money.

The Formal Call Center

The formal call center produces revenue and is characterized by large, focused groups of agents providing customer service. Formal call centers typically have one supervisor for every 12 to 14 agents, and these supervisors move frequently from one agent station to another. When not moving rapidly about, they are at their desks monitoring agents or taking .overflow and escalated calls themselves.

This type of call center requires sophisticated CTI applications, reporting, networking, and intelligent peripheral devices. Formal call centers also typically have mobile technical support personnel responsible for repairing and servicing the telecommunications and PC equipment at agent stations. Administrative staff walk frequently about the floor, seeking out agents to discuss various issues such as benefits, schedules, equipment, specific calls, and other routine administrative questions. Other than for training and breaks, agents rarely leave their desks by design; the administrator comes to the agent.

The Informal Call Center

Informal call centers are the fastest-growing segment of the call center market and are stereotypically described as customer service, order-entry, and technical assistance groups or departments. Informal call centers have the same supervisory and managerial roles as the formal call center, although the informal call center tends to be smaller with agents having a more empowered role in the call.

The informal call center often requires and has sophisticated CTI applications, enterprise connectivity, and agent access to databases, plus a variety of other information resources. Supervisors and managers are almost always available in the event of call escalation.

Though still very much tethered to their stations, these agents are typically more mobile than formal agents, although their mobility requirements are rarely more than accessing nearby resource material (e.g., in a local filing cabinet shared by several agents). Now, CTI-based screen and call transfer applications become critical tools in the call process as agents and knowledge workers transfer, conference, or continue conversations over longer periods of time. Often because answers and resources, such as documentation, reside on other workstations and sites.

The Knowledge Worker

Knowledge worker-based call centers are typically human resources, marketing groups, help desks, product support lines, and technical support staff environments. Smaller than both the formal and the informal call center, this type of call center tends to have agents who are highly educated and have not only broad access to sophisticated and specialized databases, but also to specialists and resources away from their desks or stations.

The knowledge worker agent is highly mobile, moving frequently through labs, product testing and repair areas, and seeking out engineers and other persons with subject matter expertise. A nursing station at a busy hospital is an excellent example of the knowledge call center. Caller issues are resolved usually over a series of multiple calls and callbacks, and the agent develops long-term, intimate relations with the customer.

Remote Agent/Home Office

The small office- and home office-based agent is an emerging call center segment that has surpassed 20 million, and its presence is definitely increasing. The single-site, remote agent location accounts for a substantial percentage of this growth.

By the end of the decade, one-half of the people in the United States are expected to work out of their homes. As far as call centers go, however, these remote, small office/home office agents will have little need for sophisticated transferring, queuing, conferencing, reporting, and other typical ACD features available from a call center-based environment. Some skill-set transference will be needed as call center expertise in the area of networking will benefit the technical requirements of home-based agents.

Managers of the first three types of call centers (formal, informal, and knowledge) will find their jobs increasingly more challenging and complex. Ten different themes are emerging that differentiate the old, tactical use of call center technology with the new strategic technologies of customer contact. Understanding these 10 technological requirements gives strategic managers an increased likelihood of articulating capably and responding to the challenges of moving safely from the narrow band of today into the middle band of tomorrow.

The Top 10 Technical Requirements of Customer Contact[6]

Requirement #10: Networking

The first time you add a device to a computer, PBX, or ACD you have a network. And while LANs are starting to adopt the characteristics of traditional voice processing systems such as ADCs and PBXs, the move toward star-shaped wiring, switched connections, shared media, and centralized control points defines the middle-band technology of customer contact. The very nature of requiring ever greater amounts of processing power and access to data resources from dispersed locations demands skills sets to manage the links among all of these technologies and resources.

Off-loading call processing requirements, reducing communication bottlenecks, linking geographically separated client/server clusters, integration of reporting from all of these different systems, and improving information access fall within the domain of networking.[7] Sun MicroSystems' slogan, "The Network is the Computer," says it succinctly. If you do not have a fundamental understanding of the transport of data over distance, you are functionally impaired before you ever hit the middle band of technology.

Requirement #9: Reliability

More than once have I heard a telecommunications person exclaim, "The phone system has been up and running for 50 years, and the data people cannot keep theirs up and running for 50 minutes." We are a culture with a very deeply imbedded expectation about the simple dial tone.

A deep cultural difference exists between the data people and the telecom people over what constitutes reliability. Data people do not think twice about taking a system down for a software upgrade. Most PBXs are down an average 15 seconds per year as opposed to the 150 hours per year a LAN may be down. The climax of the inevitable last throes of human digital evolution was the chess match between Gary Kasporov and Big Blue, with IBM's ensuing apology for the frustration of callers to access the real-time Internet observation of the match.

The successful integration of any device, system, platform, or architecture integral to the technology of stakeholder contact will have to be as reliable as dial tone. With reliability exists a crossover expectation that the telephone has created and sustained. And, for the time being, telephones will continue to have enormous advantages over PCs; which is not to say that PCs cannot become effective communications devices; they can, but at the moment, to make a PC as reliable as a phone is just too expensive.

Requirement #8: Object-oriented Computing

Objects are chunks of software that empower application designers to rapidly change and deploy applications to meet evolving needs without needing the MIS department. Object-oriented computing customizes icons and objects that launch, control, and intelligently coordinate other applications, databases, and communications systems.

An application is developed using the point-and-click selections from a set of building blocks that represent basic transaction functions. The blocks from a "tool-kit" of building block icons representing functions are arranged using a palette and connected in an appropriate logical sequence to facilitate the smooth flow of the transaction. The blocks are arranged graphically (visually) and connected in the appropriate logical sequence to facilitate the smooth flow of the transaction. The application is built in layers of increasing detail, giving the developer a clear view of the entire application as each step is added.

Benefits of GUI-based, application-generator development tools include their high speed of development, ease of use for nonprogrammers (which can be modified at any configuration level rather than at the program level only) and that they are 80 percent to 90 percent faster than traditional code level methods.

The advent of powerful object-oriented application generators is important because, for the computer illiterate population, we no longer need hard-core data people, and object-oriented computing allows for the rapid prototyping necessary to support information immediacy. The most significant benefit of object-oriented programming is the easy construction of fully functioning transaction processing services that access both client/server and mainframe legacy databases without C programming. Object oriented programing drives application development accessibility down to the "nonprogrammer" level. The Newtonization of technology is happening here particularly.

Requirement #7: Open Systems

Customers must have the freedom to connect existing infrastructures, including today's PBXs, ACDs, and data devices, into the emerging world of broadband, multimedia communications. Individual components of the call center will be developed using the "best of breed," "off the shelf," industry standard's components. Because CTI applications are expensive and time-consuming to build within proprietary legacy environments, the open platform of the future will allow for accelerated development.

Open architecture insures nonobsolescence. All new features will be software so that upgrades, features, and functions can be installed quickly and efficiently. A suite of client/server-based software applications provides customer information management between using both telephony and computer systems integration.

Open systems can happen only with the development of standards. Standards are not just beneficial; they are imperative. Standards enable the use of systems that are less expensive and have lower vendor margins because customers can use shrink-wrapped, as opposed to home-grown, software, among other things. Open systems based on standards provide two advantages; they allow for quick adaption to unanticipated needs (information immediacy) and prevent the reinvention of the wheel.

Requirement #6: Multimedia Connectivity

Ironically, the superior call center of the future will be the one that best manages the ACD bypass, providing interactive multimedia for complete customer communications. There will be no such thing as a call; rather, it will be a contact, a mixed medium of contacts that bypasses their traditional ACD. In the past, each media type had its own medium. Data had computers, text had word processing, and voice had the telephone. Image was fax, and video was TV and VCR. Scalability no longer means how many ports but what kind of ports. This also means not ignoring the simple phone as a device of choice for the long haul.

Requirement #5: From Any Device, to Any Database, from Anywhere

The shift from dumb rotary telephones to smart information appliances gives your stakeholders smart on and off ramps into your enterprise. The ultimate device will emerge from the convergence of three appliances: the telephone, the television, and the computer.

Requirement #4: Unlimited Bandwidth

From garden path to superhighway, the ultimate information highway will be an Autobahn of immense proportion. Asynchronous Transfer Mode-based OC3, for example, can comfortably handle the transmission, including pictures, of every issue of the *New York Times* from coast to coast in less than one second. Many large companies are already using these high-speed pipelines. If plain old telephone service is a 3-foot garden path, the broadband speeds of tomorrow will be 16 miles wide.

POTS	64,000 mph	3-ft garden path
ISDN	128,000 mph	6-ft sidewalk
T1	1,544,000 mph	4-lane road

T3	43,232,000 mph	112-lane highway
OC3	129,696,000 mph	1-mile-wide road
OC48	2,075,136,000 mph	16 miles wide

Requirement #3: Client/Server

We must move from mainframe to client/server architecture. To create customer centric, flattened, empowered, and more responsive organizations, your customers will require a more empowered and more responsive computing architecture – client/server architecture. In the future, most servers will be NT (New Technology operating system developed by Microsoft) based and clients will be Windows.

Client/Desktop Comparison, Base 1994 & 1999, in percent[9]

DESKTOP	1994	1999
Windows	63%	91%
UNIX	4	2
OS/2	5	0
Mac	12	6
Proprietary	3	1
Mainframe	1	<1
DOS	12	0

Server/Host Base Comparison, 1994 & 1999, in percent[8]

SERVER HOST	1994	1999
UNIX	16%	4%
OS/2	17	7
Netware	43	7
NT	13	81
Mainframe	1	<1
Proprietary/Other	10	1

Requirement #2: The Need for Speed

We must move from semiconductors to microprocessors. If cars developed as fast as microprocessors, the fastest cars would travel at

10,000 mph and cost $2. Never mind that these cars would only be two inches long and crash unexplainably every once in a while with a mysterious disappearance of all their occupants. Today's Nintendo games are more powerful than a 1976 Cray supercomputer. Microprocessors make possible the integration of data, text, image, and video. The $500 microprocessor of 10 years from now will have all the power of today's supercomputers with the power to provide voice processing, IVR, continuous natural speech recognition, and advanced network routing decisions – on your wrist!

Requirement #1: To Bits From Atoms

The Number One technical requirement for the technology of customer contact is the shift from analog to digital – digital technology for a digital economy. "The change from analog to digital is changing every cost curve, every investment curve, and every set of expectations about our business and our competition," Van Seidenberg, CEO of NYNEX, said in the spring of 1995. No one can say that the old way is better; if any analog proponents remain out there, they must be written off as hopelessly analog, as in anal retentive. First we saw the digitization of calls from one call center to another, and now, slowly, we see digitization emerging over the public telephone networks. As the public networks become fully digital, new kinds of call center applications become possible, such as on-line shopping and video-based agents.

Does your technology for customer contact support these 10 requirements? Probably not. Does this mean that you have legacy technology? Certainly, but pragmatism teaches that bulldozing your existing equipment is not an option either. At one time the VCR was expected to replace and eventually kill the theater business. This didn't happen because the VCR has (currently) no way to recreate the theater experience.

Conclusion

The phenomena of the middle band became very apparent to me one day when I was fighting a virus. No, I was not ill; my PC had the virus and my rent-a-genius had shown up at my home office to debug my hard drive. It turns out that my rent-a-genius did all of his programming in DOS, was marginally functional with Windows 3.1, and completely illiterate with Windows 95. I asked how much of his time he spent in Windows 3.1. "Very little," he replied. "I know DOS so well, but I know I need to start learning." He hadn't even begun to jump into the middle band of Windows 3.1, and to assume that he was already behind the curve was pretty safe.

Telecommunications and call center managers should realize that new CIO, CEO, and technology executives do not know any more about data code than they do. They think about processes and solutions, new ways of doing business. In the new world order, the only way to sell the ACD is as part of the enterprise's *infostructure* – not to integrate the ACD as a peripheral of the enterprise *infrastructure*.

In fact, the middle band, the gap of spectrum between POTS and PANS, is not going to be a smooth transition from narrow band to the broad band. If PBX and ACD technologies are considered legacy, then the onrush of client/server architecture taking over the world has been impeded by a retrofit of more than one facet of the traditional PBX and ACD. Upon closer observation, LANs are starting to look more and more like traditional PBXs, moving toward star-shaped wiring, switched connections, dedicated media instead of shared media, and centralized management and control points. On the other side of the fence, PBX-based ACDs are certainly beginning to take on characteristics of traditional LANs: server-based functionality, decentralized control, desktop controlled phones, and packet protocols.

The data people (bit-heads) are just now recognizing the following:

- the architectural strength of the star topology of the traditional PBX as the superior model for digital signal distribution;
- computer telephony integration as a technology discipline in the PBX community for more than 10 years and in the call center for almost 25 years;
- the complexity of real-time, full-duplexed voice communication and the flashback of expectations from the dial tone;
- the economic value and flexibility of switching rather than sharing media;
- superiority of the time-sensitive, cell-switching technology of Asynchronous Transfer Mode that was developed by the switch vendors for aggregate information transport.

The kink in the emergence of the new technologies found in the call center is that the process of architectural change is, first and foremost, a process of organizational change. More daunting than technology legacy is the cultural impediment left over from previous eras. The challenge of organizational change far outweighs the technological difficulties of migration from legacy systems to new technology.

Sociologists believe that people resist change because they fear the unknown. At an enterprise level the fear of cultural organizational change far outweighs the technological difficulties of migration from legacy systems to the new client/server-based technologies. Customers cling to their PBXs because PBX-based systems are less sophisticated and more "known" than the perceived sophistication of technologies like LANs. To break free from the grapple of legacy technology, the surviving PBX architecture will have a role and migration strategy based on a three-element computing model that includes the PBX architecture, the servers linking the PBX with the new technologies, and the desktop tier.

What really matters is how PBXs should evolve to harmonize with the rest of the enterprise network. The evolving call center will have to reflect open architecture, server-based design, and distributed processing and control. These new switches are designed toward not only voice communications but most other media, including voice, data, video, image, and text. These new switches will be nonblocking for all media applications and will support wireless terminals as well as wired-in terminals.

At the desktop, will the computer replace the phone? No, it will not happen for a while, but look for enhancements to existing products to support desktop multimedia applications over ISDN channels and, then, the interfacing of Asynchronous Transfer Mode and ISDN switches. Participation will be by multimedia workstation users within or across enterprises, virtual or not. The ultimate architecture will come down to issues of reliability, serviceability, and price performance.

The new enterprise is a real-time enterprise. Customer orders arrive electronically and are instantly processed, corresponding invoices are produced immediately and sent electronically, and databases are updated immediately.

To create organizations that are high performance, integrated, networked, open, and client serviced, companies need new technology that is high performance, integrated, networked, open and client/server.

The old computer model – with low-performance (traditional mainframe or mini), unintegrated (based on islands of computing), host-based (rather than networked), proprietary (nonembracing standards), and command and control (unlike client/server) computing – is the antithesis of the new technologies of customer contact.[10]

Technically savvy influencers of these technologies will insist on and recognize products with these characteristics:

- scaleable;
- open, nonproprietary architectures;

- hardware-platform independent;
- database independent;
- users of standard data communications and operating system protocols, and
- multimedia ready.

Every call that comes into the company, even if a DID (direct inward dial) call to the president, is a call that has a cost and a benefit. The role of technology is simply to maximize the difference; to lower the costs, and increase the benefits. Every call must seek these benefits. By maximizing the value of the call, you are, in turn, performing call center functions.

The benefits of the technology that meet these 10 requirements are enormous. They include eliminating the need for screening agents, reducing significantly transfers and conferences, decreasing call lengths, saving money on 800-network calls, routing calls before they are answered, enabling delivery of more personalized services, including customer preferences in your service criteria, decreasing customer waiting times, eliminating a caller's need to repeatedly restate his customer account number and call purpose, and reducing customer frustration.

The question now is, how will we achieve these benefits with the least resistance?

---

[1]Tapscott, D. (1994). *The Digital Economy*. McGraw-Hill, New York, NY, 68.
[2]Tapscott, D. (1994). *The Digital Economy*. McGraw-Hill, New York, NY, 63.
[3]Source: IVR Growth, a report by Frost & Sullivan, available April 23, 1996
[4]Halper, M. (April 8,1996). Setting up is hard to do: data warehouses do not grow on trees. *Forbes ASAP*, 50.
[5]Churbuck, D. (March 13, 1995). Help! My PC won't work! *Forbes*, 55.
[6]Letterman, D. (1996) Late Night with David Letterman. Television talk show.
[7]Distilled from an article by Allan Sulkin, BCR, June 1996, 35-36.
[8](1996). *Dataquest*
[9]Anderson, G. (1996) *Dataquest,*
[10]Tapscott, D. (1994). *The Digital Economy*. McGraw-Hill, New York, NY. 29.

GETTING TO "THERE"

Even if you are on the right track, if you are sitting still, you are going to get run over.
— Will Rogers

The Law of Life's Highway speculates that even if you are heading in the right direction but everything keeps coming at you, you may just be in the wrong lane. Many roads will lead us into the future, all with curves ahead. If you don't have a firm grip on the wheel, a clear view through the windshield, and a pretty good idea of where you are going, you are going to crash.

Anyone familiar with the technical literacy and skill sets of a 14-year-old adolescent with a Pentium-based PC that requires its own backyard cooling tower understands just how far we have come in the last few years.

Technology has permanently transformed the landscape and nature of business. Until now, this transformation has taken place almost entirely within companies and organizations, with little impact on an enterprise's stakeholders and customers. As we become an information-based society, all the related technologies of stakeholder contact and customer dialogue will change the human to machine communication paradigm from one of programming and input to one of conversation. Machines and people will communicate to solve problems faster and more accurately.

The latest paradigm shift in technology occurred when companies replaced an entire generation of clerks and low-skilled workers with the automation provided by mainframes and minicomputers.

Today, functions of white collar, deadwood middle managers in the front office are being automated through the use of desktop computing, LANs, and client/server applications. The result has been dramatic eruptions and reconstruction in many information-intensive industries including financial services, insurance, health care, and even telecommunications.

Proprietary legacy systems are giving way to integrated client/server-based systems. Developments in data bases, architectures, and client/server platforms are literally transforming the way information is structured, delivered, and used. The future of business and personal computing has become linked increasingly to the distributed, flexible, and rapidly expanding capabilities of client/server and database technologies. Management understands that to create a customer-centric, empowered, and more responsive call center, you need a more empowered, distributed, and responsive organization.

The power of interconnected people, multi-application processing systems, and multimedia information is coming from the gray area that exists between what have always been the unambiguous technologies of the public networks, customer premises equipment, and the desktop. The automation of repetitive tasks is accomplished by leveraging the integration of telecommunications technologies and LANs at the desktop.

The capability of client/server architecture underlies this transformation. Client/server architecture has emerged clearly as the dominant computing paradigm of the '90s. Virtually all of the hottest developments in personal and business computing today – JAVA, call processing, voice processing, the Internet, intranets, data warehousing, object-oriented technologies – are manifestations of client/server computing.

Today's technology of customer contact has evolved from a single big box (an ACD) with components that provide reporting, voice mail, IVR, network administration, intelligent call routing, links to host computers, and the station set itself, to a single box that is componentless. In the old systems, all the components are interlinked and hard wired rather than integrated.

As we come to adopt these client/server based technologies, the definition of a call center will increasingly become more of an issue of a mind set than anything else. From the customer's standpoint, it will mean service on demand and paying for what you use; from the provider's point of view, it will mean deploying and investing in anticipation of that customer demand.[1]

The customer of the new technology wants to move from being reactive to becoming proactive. Success will depend on predicting and acting upon these new technological opportunities before the actual need for them arises. The path of least resistance is based almost entirely on client/server computing.

The Target Customer

The pattern and trend lines have changed markedly in the new and emerging sectors of the digital technology: call centers, CTI, speech recognition, wireless, and Asynchronous Transfer Mode. Regarding telecommunication-related purchasing decisions, the telecom manager no longer has the sway he or she once had. Once a peer of the data processing manager, the telecom manager has a position that has shifted gradually to a back-office function. I envision more telecommunications departments reporting with their data networking peers up into a common management.

Increasingly, the CIO or the IS manager has become the dominant decision maker who establishes technological criteria for the convergence of telephony and computers; these managers are, in fact, convergence managers, requiring standard hardware and operating systems as well as interoperability among other information and telecom systems. Their purchase criteria for new systems incorporate the reliability requirements of telephony-grade call processing and the LAN server grade of reporting and database management.

If you have talked to a PBX vendor lately, you probably felt as if you were talking to a data guy. You are more likely to hear the words "client" and "server" rather than the familiar terms of "trunk groups" and "hunt groups."

Customers moving into this new technical paradigm share certain common attributes. One is the propensity to perform business tasks in a client/server and LAN environment, and to perform distant business tasks in a WAN environment. And, unlike in the past, most of these managers now track carefully and match the benefits of business activities to costs, which are extremely granular and detailed. These new technology managers also tend to make purchase decisions on a local or decentralized basis.

The skill sets of the convergence manager have become ever more complex. More and more, traditional telecom managers have had to become familiar with the fundamentals, structure, and functionality of LANs. In addition to needing administrative-level training on network operating systems that include network and NT Servers, these managers must also have an in-depth knowledge of the various desktop operating systems: DOS, Windows, NT, Macintosh and OS/2. Understanding middleware functionalities and integration methods is required also.[2] The complexities appear in the various decision technologies listed in Chapter Five.

Several dominant demands are emerging from these telecommunications convergence managers. The most notable follow:

- Open systems vs. proprietary systems, conforming to standards
- Smaller informal call centers vs. large call centers
- Integration of inbound and outbound systems

- More PC-based products with the shift to client/server
- Integration with work force and sales force automation.

Information Immediacy

In today's call center, seconds count. Scrutinizing work-flow details down to increments of minutes, and even seconds, can save tremendous amounts of expense.

A key element of achieving a real-time call center is capitalizing on the capability to continuously and immediately adjust your call center to changing business conditions. As a microcosm of the larger enterprise it supports, the call center, more than in any other segment of an organization, is becoming increasingly a virtual real-time enterprise, providing extraordinary caller and agent service levels through information immediacy. You cannot improve service immediacy or customer intimacy without improving accessibility.

Studies have shown repeatedly that a lack of efficiency and productivity can result directly from a lack of immediate accessibility to customer and product data in the call center. When you handle the call faster and better, you improve the customer's impression of the engagement. A good experience is intimate and sets the expectations for a repeated good experience. An extremely valuable benefit of information immediacy is the increased satisfaction of customers that results from a quicker response and resolution of their issues or questions. In the past, an "immediacy" gap was inherent in the call center station ("station" as in stationary, fixed, unmovable).

Automating those processes to support customer and stakeholder transactions that rely heavily on quick response, easy data access, and retrieval requires fast, flexible systems. Client/server fills the bill.

Client/server software-based solutions leverage the emerging integration of multiple computing and communications technologies to enable users to automate access to information and initiate action more effectively across the enterprise – all while on the telephone.

Client/Server

Client/server based software applications can manage customer information among key functional areas, using both telephony and computer systems integration. Client/server based systems are the best available means to automate business processes that rely heavily on quick response and easy access and retrieval of data for customer transactions. This type of system helps track and manage every aspect of the interactions between the company and its customers, from complete order and problem histories to prices quoted, defects resolved, special needs tracked, and sales closed. The server in the call center client/server relationship will provide two essential functions.

First, a group of functions control such things as call routing and handling, historical databases, IVR and voice processing tone recognition, network controller, and call routing. More importantly, any call center server will interface also with the PBX and with your operations' workstations, and will provide connectivity to the WAN or Internet router. A second function of the call center server will be to determine and calculate real-time status information for callers, as well as to integrate with host computer routing and network wide, cradle-to-grave reporting applications. The clients of a client/server architecture are the supervisor workstations, agent workstations, computers that run the database reporting applications, and other PC-based peripherals.

An often mistaken assumption by telecommunications managers about client/server computing is that the enterprise lacks access to legacy, mainframe-based databases. Not so. Client/server solutions can integrate effectively switch-based call processing with the mainframe computing environment, linking agent desktops with existing mainframe environments. The key is the integrating the link between the PBXs and ACD with mainframe and client/server platforms. These "links" require, of course, a fairly sophisticated skill set to develop and maintain, but the result is CTI capability that performs across products, most of the time seamlessly. The mainframe looks like a server and essentially "platforms" together with the client/server architecture.

In the past, all call center functions were accomplished on the same platform, be it stand alone or PBX based. In the future, the migration will lead to splitting functions into two or more boxes. In one plausible scenario, one box is the switch and the other is the application software. The vendors who will dominate the call center technology market over the next decade will be those who bundle their call center software as applications and repackage it in high-end servers. Often a call center will not have just one server but a family of servers. The physical cabinet will be a PC tower case, interfaced anywhere on the LAN. The PBX will finally emerge from the closet under the stairs.

As a final point, vendors are realizing that no longer can money be made off of the hardware as was the case with the legacy proprietary systems. Even the PBX and standalone vendors recognize that they should leave the bloody pricing battles to the Compaqs, Suns, DECs, and Dells (and a few peripheral industries), and that they had better get into software. The money is in the software and, although we shall not see the customer buying the software from their call center vendor and the hardware from a Digital or Compaq for the next several years, this is where the successful vendors will want to be. Over time, perhaps as few as three to five years, the ACD vendors will be unbundling their software even more so that it can run on any server box.

We shall see, possibly within three years, a rapid migration to "plugging and playing." Ultimately you should not have to buy all of your components from a single vendor. You can buy components and unify them using open interfaces with your existing database.

For now, buying an integrated product from a single vendor would be best because the platform will be "tuned" to work better with that application software than with that of any hardware system you would build yourself. In fact, buying your computing and call center infrastructure from a telecommunications vendor rather than from a data/desktop vendor, at least until after the turn of the century, is a safe idea that will not get you fired.

What would my client/server dream platform look like? My ideal call center platform architecture for the next generation, and certainly a path of least resistance, will look something like this:

- Dual Pentiums
- 128 Mb of RAM
- 22 GB RAID storage
- Windows-based supervisor desktop
- Industry standard open database
- Advanced network integration.

The future of technology for customer contact rests on client/server solutions with a LAN-based application intelligence engine. But a nagging issue hangs over client/server architectures, earned from the experiences of the past but fast being dismissed as insignificant. That issue is reliability.

Reliability

When telephony people start talking about client/server and CTI the issue of reliability invariably comes up. No call center operates acceptably only 95 percent of the time. Not being able to handshake with 5 out of 100 of your stakeholders when they contact you is disastrous. The technology of customer contact must work perfectly, all the time. To deliver less than 15 seconds of system downtime per year is no trivial exercise. To the data world, guaranteeing 15 seconds a year (one-millionth of one percent) of downtime puts a lump in most (IS) technology managers' throats, and the issue is often left untouched.

Reliability has always been a critical issue in the call center. Call centers are highly abusive to telecommunications equipment, particularly, to headsets and handsets. Every component of the call center architecture, telephone station sets especially, must be extremely durable and designed for the rigors of heavy use (abuse?).

Would call centers tolerate having their agents re-boot their phones every so often? Hardly. The reliability of the workstation has not evolved to that of the phone system, and we can safely bet that the phone will not be moving onto the PC anytime soon.

From a historical standpoint, data processing hardware has not had the reliability of telecommunications systems. However, as the reliability of the switch is being added to the data topology, the servers are becoming almost as reliable as the PBXs.

The next generation of servers in the call center will be able to process calls to stations and through applications. The reliability will come from the fact that, should functionality of the server be lost, call-processing functions will be switched over to the stable functions of the PBX-based component of the call center.

When it comes to reliability, the PBX vendors have tremendous expertise. As servers are used increasingly for mission-critical application platforms, infusing the reliability of the PBX based-systems seems to be a very practical application of the expertise of PBX/ACD vendors.

CTI in the New World Order

Computer telephony integration in the new world order will be designed by software solutions that leverage the emerging integration of multiple computing and communications technologies. These enable stakeholders, while on the telephone, to automate accesses to information and initiate resolutions more effectively across the enterprise. Required now are software and platforms that orchestrate the process by facilitating communications between voice and data environments, cross-referencing call source and destination information with the existing database identification schemes, routing calls and data to the appropriate place, and tracking processes with associated activities.

In the call center, CTI effectively integrates switch-based call processing with the mainframe computing environment, creating solutions that bring in client/server applications and link agent desktops with the existing client/server and mainframe environments. The CTI software acts on its decisions by initiating and coordinating actions: launching and controlling applications such as faxing, e-mailing, paging, and scheduling.

Basically, CTI is the catchall term that describes any number of integrated processes, including the initiation of complex, multistep actions during a call. As far as agents are concerned, selection and retrieval of information must be highly automated so the process does not distract from the conversation.

When a customer phones, to quickly pluck from mountains of distributed data precisely the information needed to serve that customer at that moment is not a trivial task. In the past, most agents have been unable to fully leverage their data for competitive benefit because the information was buried in various databases that were, in effect, hidden from many who could benefit from their use, and because the data were difficult to access. Integrating voice switching with data architectures, and taking call control instructions from the switch and translating them across a TCP/IP network to Ethernet switches, allows real-time setup of multimedia sessions that synchronize voice, data, and graphics.

Computer telephony integration has earned a place among technology disciplines, and its influence will certainly grow for several more years. Dataquest predicts that that more than 14 percent of LANs and PBXs in existence today will be integrated by year's end. Dataquest expects the CTI market to grow from $1 billion in revenues in 1995 to almost $7.5

billion by 1999.[3]

But I predict that CTI, shortly after the turn of the century, will slip into ubiquity as a discipline and, like voice or IVR, will simply become a component-like commodity. Probably not too long after Harry Newton has made off into retirement with his millions, I suspect that CTI will have melded into something far larger and more digital.

Objectives CTI

Regardless of the type of call center – formal or informal, knowledge worker or remote agent – stakeholders and customers expect service quality with every question, transaction, inquiry, and request. The ideal objective is to provide world-class service by eliminating customers' chief complaint with call centers: having to identify themselves and their problem multiple times as they are transferred throughout the organization, waiting on hold while reference information is researched, and eventually receiving an answer to a question that the customer thought the company should have given instantly.

Having the technology and the resources available to instantly present this information to the agent means that the support person can concentrate immediately on providing assistance. Before CTI, the service agent had to gather data about the call and caller first, find it on the computer, review it, and finally start to help the caller. Because of the available intelligence in the routing and processing of calls as well as the intelligent integration of technical resources, a caller no longer has to repeat who he is and why he is calling every time a call is made or is transferred to another person in your company. While call centers benefit from "screen pop," the real CTI benefit is transferring screens. The real application time-saver is in the concept of "follow-me data" or hot transfer – transfer of not only the call but also of the data that accompanied the call.

As a rule, by the time he or she has thanked the customer for calling, an agent should know who the caller is and the general nature of the call.

Depending on the completeness of the customer's file, the agent may have also comprehensive information about the customer's other related products and life-style choices. By recording and tracking details on every "touch" and transaction that occurs with every customer throughout the enterprise, a high-tech call center solution management system for the enterprise-customer relationship is formed, coordinating customer interactions across widely diverse media.

How realistic is CTI as a functional element in improving customer service? Used correctly, CTI can be extremely realistic. If used correctly, expect CTI as a functional part of the technology of customer contact to accomplish the following:

- Increase agent and supervisor productivity
- Improve caller service
- Speed information immediacy and accessibility
- Enhance competitiveness
- Streamline operations
- Improve coordination
- Facilitate instant access to information
- Yield fast response to problems, and
- Raise agent morale.

Applications Managers, A New Breed (Apart?)

The new application managers must make and judge decisions regarding server-based application software that often includes business process automation software, which is used to automate a broad range of complex, multistep, cascaded processes. A typical technical support work group would employ various common technologies and systems:

- a Lotus Notes-based help desk application
- an Oracle database application (could also be Sybase or any other brand)
- Skyword, a DOS application that automates paging
- a communications link to the InterNet

- business process automation software that integrates the support technician's use of other technologies and systems.

Like project managers, applications managers will emerge in call centers; just as product managers are responsible for their product lines, applications managers will be responsible for the application(s).

Applications managers use tools and decision oversight to monitor and control the operation and use of systems and software. This includes not only monitoring applications for failures or problems but engaging in day-to-day maintenance activities such as license management, task-flow metering, as well as software distribution and version control. Developing processes and tools for the "end-to-end" management of information from the networks and systems throughout the enterprise will be necessary and critical. As CTI-related applications become more sophisticated, the ability to monitor, troubleshoot, and optimize systems and their software (from anywhere in the network) will be a critical differentiator between a successful implementation and a losing implementation.

What will separate a successful applications manager from a failure will be the ability to evaluate objectively any particular application. In a world where technologists continuously substitute activity for achievement in the interest of job security, this new role will be fulfilled by individuals who can observe customer and stakeholder call flows, contact activities, and responses at an almost abstract level, above the technology. Many of the re-engineering processes people have gone through over the past decade have not borne fruit because they have minimized the number of steps required to do what they have always done instead of asking why they are doing it in the first place.

Computer telephony integration and its distant uncle, business process automation (BPA), are examples of technology and processes that have often failed before they have even been implemented. You must step back at the start of any technology implementation process and ask, "What are we trying to accomplish? What is the goal here?" Otherwise, you may simply be paving the cow path. And the snazzier the applications and the more integrated systems become, the more difficult it becomes to pull out.

When walking on the cow path, you must watch where you step (e.g. cybercrap). Be cautious of technology sales people peddling BPA software in the call center. The trap with BPA is the same as that of CTI: that is, you are often just automating the same mistakes you have always been making and often just end substituting activity for achievement. This has been a wake-up call to IS managers who realize suddenly that all this time they have simply been making the same mistakes, just faster and better. A key skill and aptitude of the new applications manager will be the ability to identify the right path – and not the cow path.

The Convergence of Workflow With Callflow

The results of CTI have always sounded suspiciously like those of BPA, only with the telephone thrown in. Business process automation is an emerging software technology used to make information more accessible to workers. This new class of software adds value to business processes by automating access to information in real time for users who typically conduct their business by phone. Such users include not just sales and support groups but executives, managers, and a wide variety of knowledge workers.

Software for BPA applies predetermined rules to decide whether or not any action is needed, unless established by the user. For example, if a customer accessed your company's WWW site to obtain technical support, his name and phone number could be solicited and then transferred into a call center customer data base for a predictively dialed, proactive contact.

Business process automation software includes CTI technology, which provides the architectural framework for linking computer-based applications and phone systems. So real-time call processing can be controlled by the server; but if a call or contact belongs in the business process task flow, the call can be handed off to a BPA server using sophisticated rules-based intelligence.

The crux of the client/server technology is that you are centralizing some resources and you need to be able to control whether the databases are centralized and need to be shared, or whether an application process needs to be shared by different users. Mix and match. You have a bunch of servers being shared by a bunch of clients and they bounce around. So, too, the customer's connection can bounce around as well, from each side of the call.

The customer can define the rules by which your PCs retrieve information from databases, launch and navigate applications, and interact with fax machines, e-mail, printers, pagers, voice processing, and other communications systems. This requires complex, repetitive, multistep office tasks, including many that are related to phone activity.

Reports

Peter Drucker has long complained that the modern tools produce a Niagara Falls of data while failing to deliver a useful drink of information. The volumes of information created by the technology of customer contact support this observation.

Reports are the lifeblood of call centers. In-depth call analysis enhances agent effectiveness and clearly reduces the number of call transfers, call holding times, and call backs encountered by most callers during the service cycle.

The problem with the complexity and sophistication of overflow calls between call centers is that the statistics and reports can be difficult to comprehend and difficult to find help for. But the danger with current reporting is information overload. Clear understanding is needed of how to diagnose through the interpretation of call center data.

The metrics of caller satisfaction are changing. No longer germane are average speed to answer and other 'reader board' level streams of information. The advanced call center will use the quality of dialogue, intimacy of customer conversations, and speed of actions and resolutions to measure success.

Many managers will look at their call centers and think their agents are busy – they are handling many calls. But look beyond that and ask what results from the calls – not just whether they are short or long or numerous, but what happens. As a result of a call, does caller satisfaction or increased sales or revenue result?

In response, the reporting systems from most leading PBX vendors and manufacturers of specialized ACD systems now let users slice and dice data in hundreds of customized ways and present them in beautiful graphical form. These new levels of reporting should result from the opening switch architectures to TCP/IP networking protocols so that access to management reports can be had by anyone on the corporate network, even on different corporate LANs.

A vital requirement of the next generation's call center will be the ability to provide supervisor log-in from anywhere on the WAN. With reports across the WAN, supervisors can now remotely monitor agent calls and trunk lines and allow clients to monitor their applications and campaigns from any remote touch-tone phone. To make this level of access a reality will most certainly include windows-based supervisor desktops as well as integration to standard open databases.

The call center server's internal database log that records every event that occurred on any particular call will provide critical support for reporting requirements. Events such as incoming calls and phone off-hook are communications driven. Other associated data to be logged will include the ANI, Caller ID, and prompted digits (e.g., a customer's number).

Wireless

Two types of wireless influence the future of the call center; both are significant. One, the consumer wireless market, consists of pagers, cellular phones, wireless laptops, and so on. The other is the use of wireless systems for agent mobility in the call center. We shall look at the impact of the consumer market first and then look inside the call center.

During the early stages of wireless history, mobile communications were addressed with four main devices: the cellular telephone, the residential portable telephone, the pager, and the two-way radio. Each offers different advantages in different markets, and each will impact distinctively the patterns and traffic volume of calls from your customers and stakeholders.

The increasing population of portable phones will create millions of additional points of customer access. The personal communications market is on the verge of exploding.

Carriers of PCS plan to offer hand-held wireless telephones that use digital technology much more powerful and sophisticated than do older, analog systems of the cellular networks. The PCS technology will transform the wireless phone into a mass consumer product and will eliminate cellular users' biggest gripes – dropped calls, interference, and theft of service.

Instead of waiting until I get to my office or home to call you, I am now empowered by cellular and PCS systems with instant two-way communications. This new level of accessibility equates to on-the-spot service that, in the real-time enterprise, depends on information immediacy and drives even greater levels of caller service, an extremely valuable benefit.

Wireless portable systems will have also a significant role inside the call center. With management focusing on better service levels and information, using wireless communication systems to achieve even greater degrees of information immediacy is becoming a driving factor in the success of those call centers. Improving the accessibility of agents and information in the call center is a critical element that has been identified as the ideal beneficiary of the merging of these two technologies, PBX-based call processing and a wireless communication system in the call center.

The formal, informal, and knowledge worker types of call centers are characterized by ceaseless activity. Agents, supervisors, managers, administrators, technical support staff, and other personnel never stand still – why should their telephones? When employees have to move around, the communication link is broken and productivity suffers. Studies have shown that, in dynamic call centers, supervisors and administrators are away from their desks at least one third of the time and, in the case of technical support staff, even more often.

Development of the simple headset was one of the most significant advances in the technology of call centers. The first headsets looked exactly like telephones and were strapped to an agent's ear, but, because of the Bell monopoly, not much innovation occurred until the early '70s, when headsets began to change through the use of plastics. Headsets became lighter, more comfortable, less expensive, and durable. The benefits to agents were enormous, and productivity increased dramatically.

Unfortunately, for more than 20 years, innovation has been slow in expanding an agent's workspace from the tethered four or five feet surrounding his or her station. Roaming supervisors were always looking for a place to plug in or a station to use to perform their work, such as monitoring. For supervisors and managers who need to roam, a portable station set (note the oxymoron) would be a resource dream come true.

In essence, the solution of mobility contributes to the emergence of the new type of call center – the "virtual" call center, composed of agents who traditionally could not use the phone when they were in transition between telephone-related events. Armed with mobility, the agent of the year 2000 will see the times for information transactions, wait times, and wrap-up shrink dramatically. Although the wireless technologies are here, the impediment to their implementation will certainly be cultural, not technical. In work environments where workers can be seen at their desks, managers and supervisors will have difficulty letting go and trusting that their employees are working, even while walking down the hall to the restroom!

The practical application of diverse technologies, such as a wireless communication system in the call center, easily justifies the cost because accessibility produces measurable results:

- absolutely no airtime charges
- static-free conversations
- no interference or fading
- no dropped calls
- no eavesdropping or carryover conversations
- long battery life and few power problems, and
- no radio-frequency licensing requirements.

The opportunity for solutions creating call center mobility is timely. Just as with headsets, portable handsets have increasingly become lightweight, compact, and easy to carry. The new generation of proven wireless portable telephones will fast become an advantageous strategic tool.

An extremely valuable benefit derived from portability in the call center is the increased customer satisfaction from a more immediate response and resolution of issues or questions, particularly in the informal and departmental call centers. Now customer satisfaction is achieved more often through immediate, engaging, and intimate dialogue.

Wireless mobility empowers managers and supervisors to take care of business and still be accessible. The psychology of the call center has proved that when supervisors, team leaders, and managers spend more time on the floor coaching and monitoring agents in real time, agent performance and morale improves dramatically. In addition to productivity and morale, call centers will see dramatic improvement in the operational performance and efficiency of the managers and supervisors themselves. Wireless mobility provides instant contact between agents, callers, and supervisory personnel. Wireless solutions go right to the heart of the immediate information enterprise.

Wireless solutions can further enable supervisors to provide quickly needed back-up answering positions during spikes of peak call traffic or immediate availability for calls from customers who have requested that their calls be escalated above the agent level. Eliminating or limiting on-hold waiting times during transfers for escalation calls equates to faster, better caller service. Quick problem solving is an element of achieving immediacy in the call center.

With a mobility solution, supervisors are accessible to agents and can be reached anywhere on the call center floor, instantly. No longer is trying to locate and contact people who have just stepped away from their desks an issue. Instant two-way communication equates to on the spot service which, in the real-time enterprise that depends on information immediacy, drives even greater levels of caller service.

At a higher level, supervisors in call centers are most effective when they are actively "walking the floor," maintaining rapport and involvement with the agents for whom they are responsible. Frequently though, supervisors and managers spend a significant amount of their time tied to their desks monitoring calls, taking escalated calls, or even taking overflow calls. Anyone familiar with the call center environment is aware that effective managers move around and "work the floor," interacting with agents and staff. Too often though, these very mangers and supervisors are anchored to or in motion to their desks, taking calls and resolving caller issues from their phones.

Consider wireless portability enhancing the operation of many of the administrative functions that surround and are required by a call center. Shipping and receiving, the mailroom, maintenance, security, and particularly, technical support personnel are teams and groups that are inherently mobile and available, by extension, to communicate effectively not only with outside callers but with other inside support persons.

Obviously each type of call center would have a different need for mobile communications. In the formal call center, supervisors, administrators, and technical support personnel need mobility. The informal call center would enhance the productivity of supervisors and of agents, who frequently reference local material not readily available within the radius of their phone cord. Knowledge worker environments would benefit from a large area or campus deployment of personal wireless devices. Remote Agent/Home Office is still too new a market to benefit from the power and features available on an industrial system, but benefits from cordless or hybrid cellular phones are obvious.

In essence, the technology of wireless-based mobility creates a new fifth class of call center, the "virtual" call center, composed of agents who traditionally could not use the phone when they were in transition between telephone-related events. Mobility permits agent supervisors, team leaders, and managers to cover more ground, answer questions more quickly, and make faster decisions – simply put, turning walk-away time into walk-around time.

Future Migration

Customer-intimate companies do not sell products at the leading edge. Their businesses depend on a stream of products that represent evolutionary – not revolutionary – change. Both vendors and customers should focus on delivering what their customer-intimate clients prefer – steady, controlled, incremental evolution of product, coupled with expertise that lead the clients through changes in their applications and managements.[4]

Like the sticky, resinous soot that builds up in a fireplace after years of use, and like the business re-engineering phenomenon of the last decade, most companies have piled on top of their products and services layer upon layer of services to address clients' limitations in using those very products and services. The older generations of systems were made up of not very efficient, discreet platforms that were never designed to be integrated with each other.

Call centers are upgrading constantly. A recent study found these indicators:

- 16 percent have upgraded in the past 12 years[5]
- 64 percent have upgraded in the past 1 to 6 months, and
- 20 percent have upgraded in the past 6 to 12 months.

The new generation of call center architecture will still have a switch, but the information will reside on another type of box. One integrated platform will have one base of information that drives the reports and information to agents and others. The plumbing layer will be the PBX in the traditional sense, and the service layer will be represented by the server. As we migrate forward, the future of PBX is as another server, all boxes will be servers, and the software will be consolidated into one, bundled package.

What vendors of the smart call center technology are doing is unbundling their hardware and software, so that the software is platform-independent from the switch. When you purchase the next generation call center, software for essentially all applications will be right there in the box. Access will be a matter of paying the right-to-use fee for any particular software option and getting a key code to turn it on. The application enabling code, and the applications themselves will be turned on in the system, before shipment to you.

Today when customers want to increase functionality, they have to add another box, cabinet, or card. In the new generation architecture, you just turn "on" the application, which is already built into the box. You may have to upgrade the processor, add some memory, or maybe put in a larger disk drive, but the benefit of this strategy is that the technology investment in software will migrate through those changes and the cost is no more than implementing changes in software.

I have asked several vendors, "Will I be able to buy my own box and buy just the call center software?" The answer is yes, eventually. The smartest vendors recognize that the customer population, as a whole, is still fairly illiterate when it comes to building servers with custom specifications. Until the turn of the century, most technologists would be better off buying the system specified according to their vendor's recommendation. For the next several years, expect to buy your vendor's hardware and software together, more as a quality issue than a cost issue.

You would not want to run your call center on a Packard Bell PC, would you? The new generation of call center vendors are driven to ensure that the hardware pieces of a call center stay as inexpensive as possible because they know their customers are aware that computer hardware is changing at an unprecedented rate. A processor that is inserted into that box today will, in all probability, be obsolete next year.

Much of the cost in purchasing the new platform lies in software. So the drill becomes one of the customers getting a box, turning on the monitor, and selecting the applications they want.

How do you measure the complexity of the application? An emerging pricing model will have four basic stages. Each stage or level will have more applications than its predecessor.

The first level may include basic reports and basic routing. The next may have a larger number of skills and interfaces to the host for screen pops and host influence upon the routing. The third level may have an

221

application for real-time adherence and interfaces to a network level routing package, or networking along multiple call centers. The fourth level is deeply embedded in customer programming and unlimited support, upgrade and maintenance services.

You as the customer should be looking for a vendor who prices solutions according to accommodation of the number of agents and number of applications that are turned on. The complexity of the applications as well as the number of individual agents and supervisors who will use the application should also influence the pricing matrix.

No network managers working 24-hour days to keep up with demands of distributed client/server computing and remote Internet working relish the thought of another technology migration, no matter how exciting. They know that, without the partnership of a competent vendor, technology is difficult to select, install, and integrate. The vendor is a vital factor in the equation.

The transition from legacy technologies to new architectures will be characterized by functions providing interworking between old and new, by technology that can be phased in over a period no longer than two years. A commitment should remain to continue development streams on older, legacy technology to extend and protect your existing investment as long as possible. The other side of stretching the value of your investment is to ask for attractive upgrade and economic incentives to drive systems into the new client/server architectures. The complexity of call center technologies for the coming middle-band years is that customers are demanding technology that spans obsolescence and reaches "ahead of its time."

Conclusion

We no longer have customers; we have stakeholders. Calls have become contacts. Every contact with every stakeholder has a handshake in it, usually at the beginning and the end of the transaction. There is an expression used to communicate and most often this language consists of speech and vernacular. More than just words, speech has parallel components that are further subcarriers of information. Language and the spoken word carry vast amounts of information well beyond the words themselves.

Management personnel are realizing that first impressions are everything, fast impressions are better impressions, and the ability to respond to critical calls from stakeholders and solve their problems rapidly creates a more professional image and positive call experience. Over the past several years, the call center has evolved into a powerful, integral, and crucial part of every successful organization's business equation. The technology goal in a call center is to never ever make your customer tell you the same thing twice.

Every technological advance first creates friction, obsolescence, and procrastination, and generates costs within the current environment. Operationally excellent companies can be tempted into overpricing; product leaders, into underinnovating; and customer-intimate firms, into underservicing. Balance is essential in all three disciplines to sustain market dominance.[6]

The evolution of the emerging and existing call center technologies is driven to improve productivity. Using technology to provide immediate availability of information for the agents, employees, and managers of a call center has been proven to increase productivity. Screen popping CTI applications and skills-based routing (if done correctly) are just two examples.

What do you need to service the integration intensity of the new millennium?

- fault tolerance
- 100 percent reliability
- real-time windows

- strong customer service
- real-time statistical reporting
- MIS and systems integration
- interpretation of difficult statistics
- compliance with standards

While any of these features may appear of lesser consequence, failure to deliver on any one could be viewed as a significant, even decisive, shortcoming. Likewise, excellence in any category may offer the potential of being a tiebreaker in a competitive choice situation.

Sustained product leadership comes only from a deep commitment to breakthroughs. Those ideas are not gathered at user group meetings because users want to hone and polish the product they already have. However, vendors recognize the importance of customer feedback; it helps to improve the value of existing products and extend their lives.

Tomorrow's integrated call center will have client/server technology and interfaces that access and link to applications and interface devices for call processing. Products that unify voice, fax, video, and e-mail in a single database are expected with the delivery of the next generation of mail servers from companies such as Nortel, Microsoft, IBM's Lotus, and Novell.

Smart vendors know that, even if they currently have your business, the existing customer will continue to be a challenge. Every vendor of customer-contact technology wants to be a leader in seizing new technology, but only at the right time. If you seize a new technology too early, you will have many strikeouts.

Telecommunications customers of the next century will choose a turnkey supplier who practices what he preaches and provides cradle-to-grave customer satisfaction. A brief character profile of the vendor to work with over the next five years looks like this:

- dominant market position

- large and loyal customer base
- one or more recognizable brands
- access to capital
- functional integration of its own technology, and
- strength in networking, and high-quality hardware and software.

The issue of successfully moving into, and integrating with, the technologies of customer contact in the 21st Century boils down to this: the implementation of technology must be an adaptive learning process with constant fine tuning. Technology for technology's sake is simply substituting activity for achievement.

This is just my call.

---

[1]Tapscott, D. (1994). *The Digital Economy*. McGraw-Hill, New York, NY, 257.
[2]Madsen, M. (Feb. 13,1996,). Prudential Service Company presentation. BCR PBX96 conference.
[3]Managing CTI Requires Integrated Skills, Tackett, Currid & Co., Network World, June 20, 1996
[4]Treacy, and Wiersema. (1995). *The Discipline of Market Leaders*. Addison-Wesley, New York, NY. 127.
[5](1996, March 12). CTI Expo. Pelorus Group.
[6]Treacy, and Wiersema. (1996). *The Discipline of Market Leaders*, Addison-Wesley, New York, NY., 197.